dogs

dogs

the ultimate dog lover's guide

Edward Banks

igloo

Published in 2008
by Igloo Books Ltd
Cottage Farm
Sywell
NN6 0BJ
www.igloo-books.com

10 9 8 7 6 5 4 3 2 1

ISBN: 978-1-84561-919-0

Created and designed by
THE BRIDGEWATER BOOK COMPANY

Printed in China

Photo Acknowledgments
Istock/Eric Isselée, 10, 41, 51, 59, 65, 77, 82, 95, 107, 110, 119, 121, 127, 143, 144 and 148; Istock/Mark Coffey, 11; Istock/Carl
Durocher, 15; Istock/Richard Paul, 23; Istock/James G. Charron, 28; Istock, 33, 57, 63, 85 and 156; Istock/Laila Kazakevica,
35; Istock/Nikita Tiunov, 38; Istock/Emmanuelle Bonzami, 39 and 53; Istock/Jan Bily, 42; Istock/Phillip Jones, 43; Istock/Natasha
Litova, 73; Istock/James Pauls, 81; Istock/ Brenda McEwan, 87; Istock/ Geoff Hardy, 97; Istock/Gord Horne, 99; Istock/Mark
Hatfield, 101; Istock/Doug Miller, 102; Istock/Ferenc Szelepcsenyi, 103; Istock/Lily Rosen-Zohar, 109; Istock/Ken Hurst, 111;
Istock/Annette Shaff, 117; Istock/Nikolay Titov, 123; Istock/Marcandrea Bragalini, 127; Istock/ Monika Wisniewska, 137;
Istock/Kevin Russ, 141; Istock/Brendan MacRae, 142; Istock/Graça Victoria, 145; Istock/Curt Pickens, 147; Istock/Rick Orrell,
157; Istock/Jill Fromer, 159 and Marc Henri 12, 13, 20, 21, 24, 25, 27, 29, 36, 37, 44, 45, 46, 47, 55, 58, 64, 66, 67, 71, 83, 84,
88, 89, 90, 91, 105, 106, 113, 124, 125, 129, 130, 131, 132, 133, 149, 151, 152, 153, 158.

The Bridgewater Book Company would like to thank Marc Henrie for his help and advice in researching this book.

Contents

Introduction

Before you choose a dog, you need to think about the role you want it to play in your life. Do you want a solid family pet, a jogging partner to share your love of vigorous exercise, or a tiny, cute animal that will be happy to curl up with you on the couch? Whatever your needs, there's a breed to fulfill them, and you'll find your ideal canine companion among the 100 breeds featured here.

In the chapters which follow, the breeds are divided into the broad groups in which they appear at dog shows. These mostly relate to the job the dog was originally bred for—herding dogs, terriers, toy dogs, and so on—and the fact that a dog is within a group already tells you something about it. A herding dog, hardy enough to work with sheep or cattle all day—a Border Collie, for example—is likely to need plenty of exercise and mental stimulation: you just know it won't be happy without activities to keep it busy. At the other end of the scale, a toy dog—a Pug, perhaps—bred down many generations purely as a lap dog and companion, is likely to be more demanding of human company than anything else. The last chapter in the book gives you profiles of a few of the "new" breeds—

that is, recent cross-breeds such as Labradoodles and Cockapoos, which have become so popular that they are likely to become established as independent breeds in their own right. Purists may feel that these aren't yet "true" breeds, but remember, every single dog breed in the established show categories began as a cross between two different types.

There are other factors to be taken into consideration as you make your choice, too. Some are obvious—how big does a dog grow? How much exercise does it need? But others are considerably less evident. Some breeds are much hardier than others; others aren't appropriate companions for small children. Some dogs are wonderful citizens as adults, but have a very long puppyhood and adolescence; enough to try even the most patient owner. Every breed is delightful in its own way, and every breed has the ideal owner; the information here is arranged to help you pick the profile that will match your lifestyle and ensure that your pet is as happy with you as you will be with it.

Remember to think about factors beyond the basics—as well as food, exercise and company, every dog will need veterinary care, including vaccinations and regular check-ups, and some breeds will need professional grooming. When you have the whole picture and know which dog is right for you, find a reputable breeder and "book" a puppy. It is not wise to buy from a pet store—many of their puppies come through puppy farms, which can be not only cruel but can also give you an increased chance of health and

temperament problems with your dog. Or, if you'd be happy with an adult, look up the rescue association for your chosen breed—they will have checked out any dog they offer you.

Acquiring a dog is an important decision. Each of the dogs in our breeds' list is described in detail—not only providing information on appearance as well as exercise and training requirements, but taking into account what you, as an owner, can offer. Think of it as a canine dating agency, matching you with the breed that will be just right for your home and your lifestyle.

Size, appearance, and coat sections cover the basics: a thumbnail portrait of how the dog looks.

An analysis of typical physical traits of the dog.

All breeds have some health concerns—the breeding-in of specific characteristics can also encourage a predisposition to some conditions. This section gives a realistic overview of possible health concerns specific to the breed, not to frighten you off the dog, but to make sure that you are fully informed when you talk to a breeder.

A list of the qualities you need to be a good match with this breed.

Great Dane

A look at the breed's origins and history— where and how it came into being— and a description of its broad character.

Key things you need to know about this dog's care, on a scale of between one and five pawprints. One pawprint indicates that not much exercise or grooming is needed; that it is easy to train and inexpensive to keep. Five pawprints indicates very high exercise needs, plenty of—probably professional—grooming, a demanding dog to train, and an expensive one to keep. The scale will give you an idea of what you may be taking on.

Sporting Dogs

This section contains the dogs that were originally bred to find and retrieve game—and includes pointers, spaniels, retrievers and setters, in a wide range of sizes. What most of the breeds in this chapter have in common, however, is that they are, for the most part, quite readily trained and make energetic and lively pets. Their genetic make-up means that they tend to need plenty of exercise and face-to-face time interacting with "their" humans.

Cocker Spaniel

COCKER SPANIEL FACTS

SIZE Dog, height at shoulder, 15 in (38 cm); bitch, height at shoulder, 14 in (36 cm).

APPEARANCE The flowing hair and soulful expression disguise a solid, compact little dog.

COAT The long, silky coat needs care to keep it looking good. Colors range from solid black, cream, brown or red, to two-colored varieties (any of the solid colors teamed with white).

BREED HEALTH The popularity of the Cocker Spaniel has led to overbreeding, which has resulted in a wide range of possible genetic faults. If buying from a breeder, check the background of the breeding stock.

AN OWNER NEEDS... Plenty of time for the dog's high grooming needs.

The glamorous coat of the typical Cocker conceals a lively, energetic character that originally earned its keep as a gundog ("cocker" refers to the woodcock that the working spaniel retrieved). Today more commonly found as a companion than a working dog, this mid-sized spaniel is cheerful and devoted to its family. Its exercise needs are moderate and it is generally good with children, but its coat needs a great deal of attention to keep it in top condition.

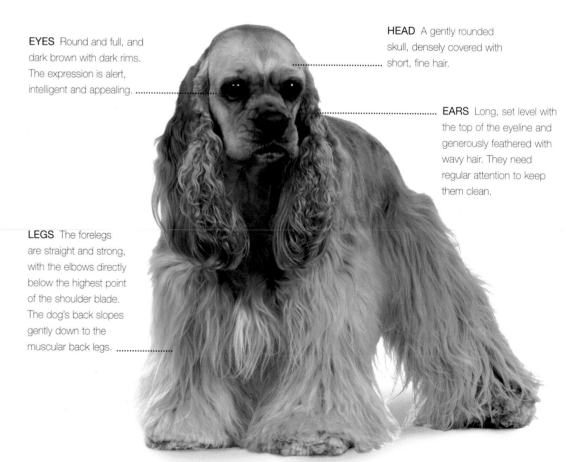

EYES Round and full, and dark brown with dark rims. The expression is alert, intelligent and appealing.

HEAD A gently rounded skull, densely covered with short, fine hair.

EARS Long, set level with the top of the eyeline and generously feathered with wavy hair. They need regular attention to keep them clean.

LEGS The forelegs are straight and strong, with the elbows directly below the highest point of the shoulder blade. The dog's back slopes gently down to the muscular back legs.

ESSENTIALS EXERCISE 🐾🐾🐾 GROOMING 🐾🐾🐾🐾🐾 EASY TO TRAIN 🐾🐾🐾 EXPENSIVE TO KEEP 🐾🐾🐾🐾

Weimeraner

Smart, energetic, and independent, Weimeraners are gundogs named for Weimar, the region in Germany in which they were developed. They make popular pets but can be hard to train because, although bright, they are not always prepared to operate to a human agenda. They need plenty of attention and exercise from a dedicated owner.

WEIMERANER FACTS

SIZE Dog, height at shoulder, 25–27 in (63–69 cm); bitch, height at shoulder, 23–25 in (58–63 cm).

APPEARANCE An active, alert-looking gundog with beautiful coloring and a neat, elegant outline.

COAT Fine, dense short coat in solid gray; shades can range from a silvery to a darker steel color.

BREED HEALTH A strong breed without many genetic health problems, but has a slight inherited tendency towards hip dysplasia.

AN OWNER NEEDS... Patience to train their Weimeraner carefully and thoroughly, plus plenty of time to spend with their dog. Weimeraners don't like to be left alone and tend to develop strong bonds with their owners.

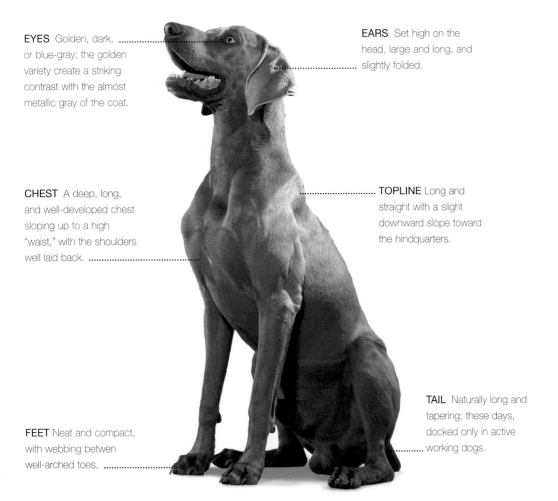

EYES Golden, dark, or blue-gray; the golden variety create a striking contrast with the almost metallic gray of the coat.

EARS Set high on the head, large and long, and slightly folded.

CHEST A deep, long, and well-developed chest sloping up to a high "waist," with the shoulders well laid back.

TOPLINE Long and straight with a slight downward slope toward the hindquarters.

TAIL Naturally long and tapering; these days, docked only in active working dogs.

FEET Neat and compact, with webbing betwen well-arched toes.

ESSENTIALS EXERCISE 🐾🐾🐾🐾 GROOMING 🐾🐾 EASY TO TRAIN 🐾🐾🐾 EXPENSIVE TO KEEP 🐾🐾

Clumber Spaniel

CLUMBER SPANIEL FACTS

SIZE Dog, height at shoulder, 18–20 in (46–51 cm); bitch, height at shoulder, 17–19 in (43–48 cm).

APPEARANCE A long, low working spaniel of solid, dignified and substantial appearance.

COAT Silky textured and very dense and flat, without curl. White coat, usually with pale lemon markings around the head, although markings of a darker tan, or "orange", color are allowed in the breed standard.

BREED HEALTH Generally good, with some instances of hip dysplasia, back problems, and ingrowing eyelashes.

AN OWNER NEEDS... The energy to accompany this dog on long walks, and to be prepared to spend extensive time grooming its silky coat.

The heaviest of all the spaniel breeds, the Clumber was originally developed by crossing the basset with a now-extinct form of spaniel native to the Alps. The name comes from Clumber Park, part of the Duke of Newcastle's estate, where these dogs were kept and bred in the early 19th century. Now a comparatively rare breed outside the shoot or the show ring, the Clumber Spaniel is an excellent working dog and makes a good-tempered, solid, and reliable pet. It does, however, need a great deal of exercise to keep it fit.

TAIL Often still docked in working dogs. If left natural, of medium length and carried level with the line of the dog's back, or slightly higher.

TOPLINE A long, strong neck descending in a slight curve to a straight, broad, level back.

EYES Dark amber in color and deep-set in a diamond shape, with a rather mournful expression that belies the dog's confident and cheerful temperament.

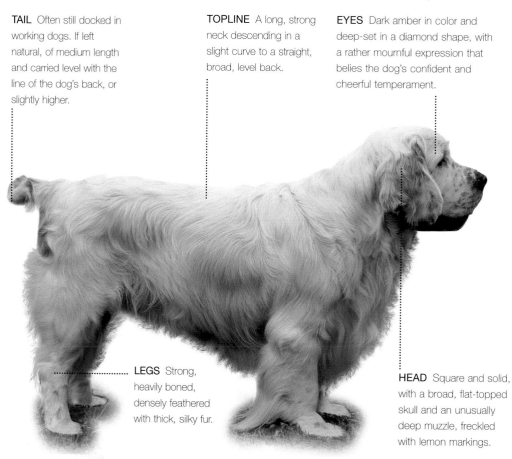

LEGS Strong, heavily boned, densely feathered with thick, silky fur.

HEAD Square and solid, with a broad, flat-topped skull and an unusually deep muzzle, freckled with lemon markings.

ESSENTIALS EXERCISE 🐾🐾🐾🐾 GROOMING 🐾🐾🐾🐾 EASY TO TRAIN 🐾🐾🐾 EXPENSIVE TO KEEP 🐾🐾🐾

Chesapeake Bay Retriever

Bred in the Chesapeake Bay area of Maryland in the United States, this hardy retriever is a strong swimmer and an indefatigable worker. It is probably the result of crosses between Newfoundlands, Otterhounds and other types of retriever. Developed to hunt waterfowl, it is still much more commonly found as a working dog than a pet, although it shares the cheerful, lively, and sensible temperament of some other more generally popular retriever breeds.

CHESAPEAKE BAY RETRIEVER FACTS

SIZE Dog, height at shoulder, 23–26 in (58–66 cm); bitch height at shoulder, 21–24 in (53–61 cm).

APPEARANCE Solid and well-balanced, with a deep chest and a square head with a tapering muzzle.

COAT Double coat, with a wavy, oily outer coat and a dense, woolly underlayer, in shades of solid brown, from deep fawn to rich chestnut.

BREED HEALTH Generally healthy, but there is a tendency to degenerative myelopathy, a disease that affects the function of the back legs. Check before acquiring a dog that the breeder's stock has been cleared.

AN OWNER NEEDS... "Chessies" do well in obedience and field trials, but have plenty of energy and need to be kept busy, with regular and plentiful exercise.

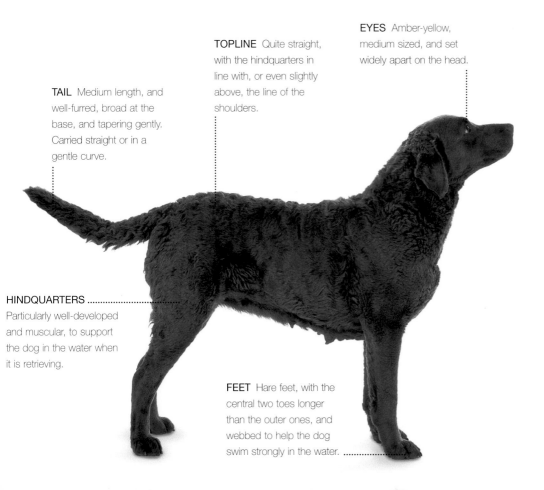

EYES Amber-yellow, medium sized, and set widely apart on the head.

TOPLINE Quite straight, with the hindquarters in line with, or even slightly above, the line of the shoulders.

TAIL Medium length, and well-furred, broad at the base, and tapering gently. Carried straight or in a gentle curve.

HINDQUARTERS Particularly well-developed and muscular, to support the dog in the water when it is retrieving.

FEET Hare feet, with the central two toes longer than the outer ones, and webbed to help the dog swim strongly in the water.

ESSENTIALS | **EXERCISE** 🐾🐾🐾🐾 | **GROOMING** 🐾🐾🐾 | **EASY TO TRAIN** 🐾🐾🐾 | **EXPENSIVE TO KEEP** 🐾🐾

Golden Retriever

GOLDEN RETRIEVER FACTS

🐾 **SIZE** Dog, height at shoulder, 23–24 in (58–61 cm); bitch, height at shoulder, 21½–22½ in (54–57 cm).

🐾 **APPEARANCE** A substantial, symmetrical, active retriever, with a balanced and elegant outline.

🐾 **COAT** Double coat, with a substantial, water-repellent outer layer and a close-lying, softer undercoat. The coat is of medium length, and may be straight or have a slight wave; the color, as the name suggests, is solid gold, although the range may go from a light, creamy gold to a very deep golden-yellow hue.

🐾 **BREED HEALTH** Generally healthy, but some genetic predisposition to hip dysplasia, elbow dysplasia, and a variety of eye conditions.

🐾 **AN OWNER NEEDS...** To obtain a puppy from a reputable breeder, and to check that their breeding stock has been screened. Ill-bred Golden Retrievers can be bad-tempered or hard to train. This is an energetic breed that needs regular outings, training, and plenty of exercise.

Despite one romantic tale that holds that the Golden Retriever is descended from a troupe of Russian circus dogs, the more mundane truth is that it was developed on Lord Tweedmouth's Scottish estate in the mid-19th century, from a mix of retrieving and spaniel stock. The result was more successful than its breeders dreamed: a surpassingly popular pet and companion dog that remains useful and active in its original hunting role.

One of the most attractive of the retrieving breeds, the Golden Retriever's flowing, wavy coat, kind, level gaze, and *joie de vivre* quickly won it a wide fanbase outside the sporting world. From its first registrations with the American Kennel Club in 1894 and the Kennel Club of England in 1903, its popularity grew fast. Its calm and level-headed temperament quickly proved the breed to be very suitable for training as a guide dog and for search-and-rescue work .

Yet Golden Retrievers can be extremely boisterous as puppies, and some have a long adolescence, lasting well into their third year. Also, the popularity of this breed has left it open to exploitation and breeding for profit; for this reason, it is extremely important that anyone considering one of these dogs goes to a reputable breeder or even to a rescue organization that checks its

dogs: only by this means will some of the poorer strains eventually be bred out. The well-bred adult Golden Retriever is lively but attentive—energetic, playful, and very good-natured.

Naturally high-spirited, Golden Retrievers are also keen to please and will respond well to training, although patience may be needed on the part of the trainer to get ideas into the head of an intelligent but excited and somewhat hyper Golden Retriever puppy. This breed usually gets along with everyone—it is affectionate with its owners, friendly and playful with children, and easygoing with both familiar and unknown dogs and other pets.

As might be expected from a waterfowl retriever, this dog adores playing in water and needs regular exercise. Owners should be prepared to give it regular and lengthy walks.

EYES Oval in shape and rather large, usually dark brown, although lighter shades of hazel are sometimes seen. The rims around the eyes are always dark.

EARS Fixed just above eye level, very mobile at the base, and falling slightly forward alongside the dog's cheeks.

HEAD Well-shaped and broad at the top of the skull, with a clear stop between the upper face and the muzzle. The latter is wide and quite long; the nose is large and should be black or very dark brown.

CHEST Well developed and deep but not particularly broad, with a moderate "tuck-up" behind the ribcage, giving the dog a pronounced "waist."

TOPLINE Level from the base of a strong neck, with a very slight downward slope just before the tail.

TAIL Broad at the base and heavily feathered. Carried in a relaxed curve, slightly above the topline of the dog's back.

LEGS Muscular and well developed; the front legs straight and solidly boned, the back legs strong and moderately angled. Feet are medium size, with compact, thick pads.

● **ESSENTIALS** EXERCISE 🐾 🐾 🐾 🐾 GROOMING 🐾 🐾 🐾 EASY TO TRAIN 🐾 🐾 EXPENSIVE TO KEEP 🐾 🐾 🐾

Labrador Retriever

LABRADOR RETRIEVER FACTS

SIZE Dog, height at shoulder, 22½–24½ in (57–62 cm); bitch, height at shoulder, 21½–23½ in (55.5–60 cm). European and American strains of this breed are gradually diverging, and the American Labrador is now typically the larger of the two.

APPEARANCE This is a medium-sized, strongly built dog, with a clean-cut, handsome head and characteristic "otter" tail.

COAT A hard double coat, the top layer short, straight and thick, with a softer, very short undercoat. The Labrador Retriever is solidly colored in black, chocolate, or yellow (deep cream to reddish gold).

BREED HEALTH Generally healthy, but prone to some disorders, including hip and elbow dysplasia, muscular dystrophy, bloat, and some eye problems. Labrador puppies are widely available but should only be obtained from a reputable and established breeder, so that owners can be sure that stock has been screened for health problems.

AN OWNER NEEDS... Plenty of time for training and exercising this energetic and enthusiastic dog. Labs are not good at being left alone for long periods, and need to be treated as members of "their" families.

Today a universally widespread and popular pet, the Labrador Retriever was originally bred as a water dog and was used in its native Newfoundland to help the fishermen pull in their nets. After it was imported to England in the mid-19th century, the breed quickly became successful as a sporting retriever, working in the water and on land. This adaptable and trainable breed has worked in many roles, from guide dog to obedience champion.

It is also one of the most popular of all breeds as a family pet, and is well suited to the role. The characteristics that make it such a highly regarded working dog—an even temper, readiness to learn, and a cheerful, enthusiastic outlook—are just as valuable in a domestic situation.

Labradors are extremely lively and boisterous as puppies and can take some time—often well into their second year—to mature. Despite this, the Labrador is not usually a hard breed to train; naturally tractable and keen to please their owners, even young and very energetic Labs will respond well to consistent and positive training. This dog also makes a wonderful playmate for children big enough to withstand its advances, although it is too large and clumsy to play unsupervised with toddlers and, for the same reason, is not a good choice for anyone very

elderly who may not be strong enough to repel its well-meant onslaughts of exuberance.

Temperamentally, Labradors are not high-maintenance dogs, but they are very active, and also have a tendency to put on weight—almost all Labs love to eat. As a result, keeping this breed well-exercised and its food intake within limits are key to maintaining a fit and healthy dog. Labs are extremely enthusiastic swimmers—unsurprisingly, given their origins—and will take any opportunity to "retrieve" from almost any body of water, whether it's the sea or merely a large puddle.

Today, the vast majority of Labrador Retrievers are yellow coated, although the original Labrador was solid black, and there is also a solid-chocolate-colored variety. The coat does need regular brushing, because this dog sheds quite heavily, particularly in the spring and the autumn.

EARS Moderately broad and long, an elongated triangle in shape, set far back on the head, and quite low.

EYES Rounded and of medium size, set in dark rims. Their warm, friendly expression is particularly typical of this breed.

HEAD A broad skull and a well-developed rectangular face, with a pronounced "stop"—the dividing point between the top of the face and the muzzle. Clean-cut under the eyes and around the jaw.

TOPLINE Straight and solid with a slight downward curve toward the tail.

TAIL The so-called "otter" tail is one of the defining characteristics of the Labrador and helps the dog swim strongly: very broad and wide at the base, it tapers gradually to the tip. It should be of moderate length.

LEGS Strong and solidly boned, with very developed and muscular hindquarters.

ESSENTIALS   EXERCISE 🐾🐾🐾🐾   GROOMING 🐾🐾🐾   EASY TO TRAIN 🐾🐾   EXPENSIVE TO KEEP 🐾🐾🐾

English Springer Spaniel

ENGLISH SPRINGER SPANIEL FACTS

SIZE Dog, height at shoulder, 19–21 in (48–53 cm); bitch, height at shoulder, 18–20 in (46–51 cm).

APPEARANCE A stylish, balanced, and substantial spaniel with long legs and a flowing coat.

COAT A double coat, the outer layer of medium length, straight or slightly wavy, with deep feathering on the legs, ears, and tail. The English Springer Spaniel is found in a range of colors, including black or liver with white markings, or white with black or liver markings, tricolor (which includes small tan marks), or blue-gray or liver roan (in which there is a thick scattering of white hairs alongside the main coat color).

BREED HEALTH Usually healthy, but some tendency towards hip dysplasia, allergies, and eye problems, and a susceptibility to ear infections.

AN OWNER NEEDS... Boundless energy. The English Springer is an extremely lively dog with a very high exercise requirement that may take some time to train. It also has high grooming needs—it is enthusiastic about mud and water and is very sociable—which means that it can be quite messy at home.

The English Springer is a breed with extremely ancient roots—although Springer and Cocker Spaniels were not recognized as separate breeds in the 19th century, dogs very like the English Springer appear in sporting paintings from the early 18th century. Springers were so-named because their job out hunting was to "spring" fowl from ground cover into the air so that they could be shot. Today, the English Springer is still a popular field dog.

As well as regularly excelling in field trials, working as a gundog, and serving as a successful show breed, the English Springer is a popular pet in the UK and is becoming increasingly well known in Europe and North America.

Like most field spaniels, it is an extremely energetic and lively dog that needs plenty of exercise and mental stimulation to achieve its full potential. Working dogs receive regular physical and mental workouts in the field, but the owners of domestic pets need to plan their dogs' lives to ensure that they have the same "job satisfaction" from their day-to-day lives. Many owners with pet spaniels enter them in agility, obedience, or field trials, to give the dogs the same experience enjoyed by working dogs.

The English Springer Spaniel is most suitable for a home with access to plenty of open ground; it isn't a good choice for an urban life where open spaces are rare, or for a small apartment.

This breed is fond of human company and should not be left alone for long periods—loneliness or boredom can result in a very hyper and over-excitable dog that may also become prone to recreational barking. Properly cared for, however, the English Springer can excel as a pet. It is usually fond of children, and seems inherently to understand that it needs to tone down its boisterous behaviour with toddlers; it is also instinctively keen to please. As a result, even quite young puppies are attentive when being trained, although they may also be easily distracted, and training can be quite a prolonged process. Even if training is time-consuming, the springer's natural intelligence and *joie de vivre* will prevent it from becoming too much of a chore to its owner.

EYES Oval, deep-set, and of medium size, with dark rims that match the dog's coat color. The eyes themselves are brown or hazel in the lighter colors.

HEAD Well-modelled and with a pronounced stop between upper face and muzzle. The nose is black or liver, matching the colors in the coat.

EARS Long, wide and thin, with a heavy feathering of fur. Set quite low on the head, hanging well below the dog's jaw.

TOPLINE Sloping gently and evenly from the base of the neck to the base of the tail.

LEGS This is a relatively long-legged spaniel; the forelegs are set well under the relatively broad chest.

FEET Solid and oval, with thick, close-set pads suitable for covering rough terrain.

ESSENTIALS EXERCISE 🐾🐾🐾🐾 GROOMING 🐾🐾🐾 EASY TO TRAIN 🐾🐾🐾 EXPENSIVE TO KEEP 🐾🐾🐾

Viszla

VISZLA FACTS

SIZE Dog, height at shoulder, 22–24 in (56–61 cm); bitch, height at shoulder, 21–23 in (53–58 cm).

APPEARANCE The Viszla bears a strong resemblance to its German cousin the Weimaraner, with the same spare, muscular outline.

COAT Short, dense coat in solid shades of golden rust. The breed standard allows a small white "blaze" on the chest.

BREED HEALTH Generally healthy, but with susceptibilities to epilepsy (check breeding stock) and hip dysplasia.

AN OWNER NEEDS... Plenty of personal time to spend with this strongly devoted breed. Viszlas tend to be one-person dogs, and they like to be close to "their" person as much of the time as possible.

The Viszla hails from Hungary and bears a striking resemblance to the Weimaraner, although it is slightly smaller. It was not known outside its native country until examples were exported to other parts of Europe and to the United States (where it was first shown in 1960) after the Second World War. It is fast gaining popularity as a pet; like any breed with a recent history as a working dog, it needs careful training and plenty of exercise.

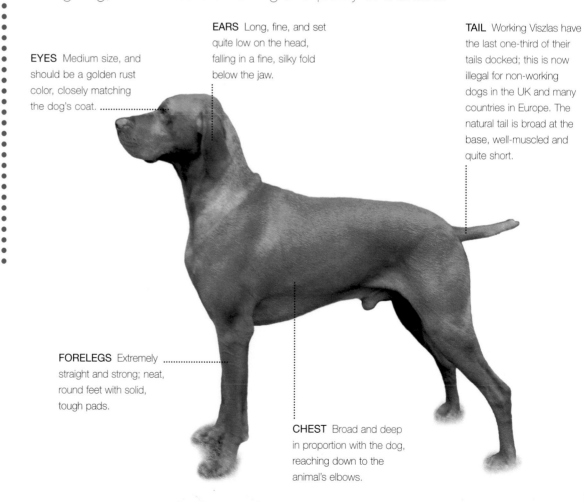

EARS Long, fine, and set quite low on the head, falling in a fine, silky fold below the jaw.

TAIL Working Viszlas have the last one-third of their tails docked; this is now illegal for non-working dogs in the UK and many countries in Europe. The natural tail is broad at the base, well-muscled and quite short.

EYES Medium size, and should be a golden rust color, closely matching the dog's coat.

FORELEGS Extremely straight and strong; neat, round feet with solid, tough pads.

CHEST Broad and deep in proportion with the dog, reaching down to the animal's elbows.

ESSENTIALS EXERCISE 🐾🐾🐾🐾 GROOMING 🐾 EASY TO TRAIN 🐾🐾🐾 EXPENSIVE TO KEEP 🐾🐾🐾

Gordon Setter

The largest of the setters, the Gordon Setter is named for the Scottish estate where it was developed—possibly by introducing bloodhound and collie blood into standard setter stock—toward the end of the 18th century. Today it is still a stalwart working dog, full of stamina and tireless in the field, but it is also kept as a pet, and is quite popular in North America. The Gordon Setter is attached to its family, although it may be reserved with outsiders. It needs plenty of exercise to keep it on an even keel and is not suited to urban life.

GORDON SETTER FACTS

SIZE Dog, height at shoulder, 24–27 in (61–69 cm); bitch, height at shoulder, 23–26 in (58–66 cm).

APPEARANCE A large, handsome, sturdy but athletic dog of typical setter appearance.

COAT Soft, dense coat, medium length, either straight or with a slight wave. The color is black with tan markings above the eyes, on the muzzle and chest, on the backs of the legs and under the tail.

BREED HEALTH Gordon Setters are generally strong, but may have some tendency to hip dysplasia and bloat.

AN OWNER NEEDS... Sufficient time to train this rather shy breed, and either to use it as a sporting dog, or to give it plenty of exercise—this is a dog that needs to be active.

HEAD Rounded at the top and very deep in the jaw, with an angular, square appearance.

TOPLINE Long, with a gentle, downward slope toward the tail.

TAIL Short for the size of dog, strongly tapered and feathered, and carried straight.

LEGS Strong, well-boned, and heavily furred with "pantaloons" of hair.

FEET The paws are shorthaired and of the "cat" type: neat and compact, with deep, thick cushioned pads.

ESSENTIALS **EXERCISE** 🐾🐾🐾🐾 **GROOMING** 🐾🐾🐾 **EASY TO TRAIN** 🐾🐾🐾🐾 **EXPENSIVE TO KEEP** 🐾🐾🐾

Irish Setter

IRISH SETTER FACTS

SIZE Dog, height at shoulder, 26–28 in (66–71 cm); bitch, height at shoulder, 24–26 in (61–66 cm).

APPEARANCE A graceful, elegant, but strong-looking dog, especially beautiful in movement.

COAT Short and fine on the front forelegs and the head; long, wavy hair elsewhere on the body. Deep chestnut or mahogany red, sometimes with small patches of white on the chest or feet.

BREED HEALTH Some genetic tendency to hip dysplasia, epilepsy, and bloat. Irish Setters can also suffer from a range of skin allergies.

AN OWNER NEEDS... Plenty of energy and time to exercise and train this very lively dog, and access to open areas where it can run freely. This isn't a suitable dog to keep in a confined space. The fine coat also calls for regular and careful grooming to keep it in good shape.

The Irish or Red Setter is one of the aristocrats of the sporting group—with its long, flowing coat in a gleaming shade of chestnut, its graceful carriage and its smooth movement, it would be hard to imagine a more beautiful dog. Yet its refined looks can be deceptive—this is a lively, naturally active and sociable breed that needs plenty of training, exercise, and personal time to keep its extensive energies in check.

As with any old breed, the origins of the Irish Setter are debated—it was already an established type by the early 19th century, and is believed to have been developed from early Scottish setters, with some pointer and spaniel in the mix. Some breeders believe that some sighthound stock, possibly Borzoi, may have been bred in later, accounting for the Irish Setter's unusually graceful and elongated lines. Early examples of the breed were red and white in color, and a variant —the Red and White Setter—with the original bi-coloring still exists, although it is very rare. By the early 19th century, the Irish Setter was well established as a particularly popular and successful hunting companion, a superlative pointer and retriever. It is still well known to hunters as a willing and untiring worker, while its beauty has ensured it is in high demand as a

show dog. Its cheerful character and natural high spirits have also made it a popular pet.

Like many other fine working dogs, it needs to be kept occupied and stimulated, both mentally and physically. For this reason, it isn't suitable for anyone who has a limited amount of space or time to offer. Underexercised or underemployed Irish Setters can go literally crazy from boredom—like that other famous worker, the Border Collie, they actually need to "work." Whether that work consists of a hard day's retrieving in the field or an hour or two of "fetch the stick" doesn't really matter—the Irish Setter will bring its boundless enthusiasm to whatever activity you suggest, and is also usually happy to run and play with other dogs. This breed can be quite slow to mature, and may continue with exuberant puppy behavior until three or four years old.

HEAD Lean and elongated in shape, with an oval-shaped top to the skull. Twice as long as the width between the ears, and delicately shaped around the muzzle and jawline.

EARS Long and set far back on the head, below the dog's eyeline. Thin and lavishly furred.

TOPLINE An even line with no sharp angles, sloping gently down toward the hindquarters.

TAIL Forms a natural extension to the topline; long, tapering from a broad base, and gracefully fringed.

CHEST Deep, but of only moderate width, so as not to interfere with free forward movement.

HINDQUARTERS Well-developed, strong, and powerfully muscled; this dog is renowned for its stamina among sporting breeds.

ESSENTIALS EXERCISE 🐾🐾🐾🐾🐾 GROOMING 🐾🐾🐾 EASY TO TRAIN 🐾🐾🐾 EXPENSIVE TO KEEP 🐾🐾🐾

Brittany

BRITTANY FACTS

SIZE Dog, height at shoulder, 19–21 in (48–53 cm); bitch, height at shoulder, 17–19 in (43–48 cm).

APPEARANCE Neat and compact, this dog looks more like a small retriever than a spaniel.

COAT Thick, medium in length, smooth or slightly wavy, in orange and white, or liver and white. A black-and-white version is accepted in the UK, but not in the US.

BREED HEALTH Strong, healthy, and often long lived, but with a small susceptibility to epilepsy and hip dysplasia.

AN OWNER NEEDS... Plenty of face-to-face time for this affectionate dog, plus the energy for lengthy daily walks. A good deal of exercise will keep it on an even keel.

Known in the past as the Brittany Spaniel, this dog probably originated in northern France or Spain, and was developed as a sporting pointer and retriever. Its outgoing temperament and friendliness have made it a popular pet in recent years, and it is a good companion dog. It needs plenty of exercise, however, and is also not usually happy to be left alone. It is intelligent and lively, but has the reputation of being somewhat slow to train.

HEAD A marked stop gives the Brittany a resemblance to the retrieving breeds.

TOPLINE A very straight back leads from a solid, well-muscled neck.

TAIL Brittanys often have tails that are naturally very short—4 in (10 cm) or less. If longer, the tails of working dogs are still sometimes cropped.

LEGS Lightly feathered with hair (the ears also have a slight fringe).

ESSENTIALS EXERCISE 🐾🐾🐾🐾🐾 GROOMING 🐾🐾🐾 EASY TO TRAIN 🐾🐾🐾🐾 EXPENSIVE TO KEEP 🐾🐾

Irish Water Spaniel

This large, unusual-looking, curly-coated dog has been acting as a water retriever in its homeland since the mid-19th century. Intelligent and very energetic, it is first and foremost a working dog that can successfully combine this role with that of family pet. An active breed that needs a good deal of exercise, it has also enjoyed a good record in the show ring as well as in agility and obedience classes. It is keen to please and is easy to train.

IRISH WATER SPANIEL FACTS

SIZE Dog, height at shoulder, 22–24 in (56–61 cm); bitch, height at shoulder, 21–23 in (53–58 cm).

APPEARANCE A solid, good-looking outline reminiscent of the Standard Poodle, with an eager, bold expression.

COAT A thick covering of dense, Poodle-like curls in deep liver, with a softer undercoat all over, except on the muzzle and tail.

BREED HEALTH Careful breeding has given this dog an excellent health record and inherited tendencies or conditions are rare, but there are some instances of hip dysplasia and skin problems.

AN OWNER NEEDS... Sporting work for this dog to do, or the inclination for plenty of exercise. As expected, these dogs adore swimming.

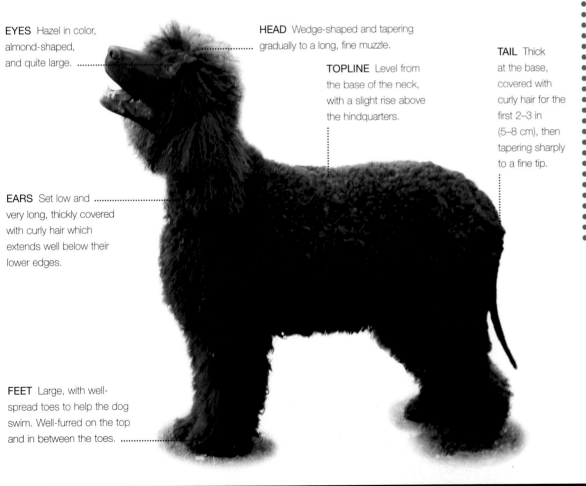

EYES Hazel in color, almond-shaped, and quite large.

HEAD Wedge-shaped and tapering gradually to a long, fine muzzle.

TOPLINE Level from the base of the neck, with a slight rise above the hindquarters.

TAIL Thick at the base, covered with curly hair for the first 2–3 in (5–8 cm), then tapering sharply to a fine tip.

EARS Set low and very long, thickly covered with curly hair which extends well below their lower edges.

FEET Large, with well-spread toes to help the dog swim. Well-furred on the top and in between the toes.

ESSENTIALS EXERCISE 🐾🐾🐾🐾 GROOMING 🐾🐾🐾 EASY TO TRAIN 🐾🐾 EXPENSIVE TO KEEP 🐾🐾🐾

German Wirehaired Pointer

GERMAN WIREHAIRED POINTER FACTS

SIZE Dog, height at shoulder, 24–26 in (61–66 cm); bitch, height at shoulder, 22–24 in (56–61 cm).

APPEARANCE A large, muscular pointer with an active, balanced build, a weatherproof coat and characteristically lavish mustache, beard and eyebrows.

COAT A wiry topcoat with a short undercoat that is largely shed in summer. The density of the fur varies over the body, being noticeably thicker in the ruff around the neck. Colors are liver and white or solid liver, with some variations in different markings.

BREED HEALTH Generally a sturdy and healthy breed, with occasional tendencies to hip dysplasia, epilepsy, and some eye problems.

AN OWNER NEEDS... To be able to give this dog an active, interesting life, whether or not it works, and to be tolerant of its constant need for company: the Wirehaired Pointer is well known for "shadowing" its owner, following his or her every move. Apart from its exercise requirement, this is not a dog that makes very high demands on its owners.

The German Wirehaired Pointer is a comparatively recent breed, created just over a century ago, probably by crossing various scenthounds with the Wirehaired Pointing Griffon, an energetic but now scarce gundog originating in Holland. Its outline is similar to that of the German Shorthaired Pointer, and it is an effective gundog that can both "point" and follow a scent trail. It is currently more popular in Germany and North America than in the UK.

It was first registered in the UK in the 1950s, and in the United States in 1959. Like all working dogs, the German Wirehaired Pointer needs careful training to become a successful pet as well as to be a successful hunting dog. Pointers are intelligent and dependable, but can be strong-willed and this is too large a breed for an owner to allow to be undisciplined or out of control.

At home, this pointer becomes fond of its family, focusing on one person in particular, and will enjoy following the object of its affections around the house, as well as out of doors. Care should be taken that the jealous streak that some pointers display is not allowed to develop too strongly. The Wirehaired also shows no awareness of its size; indoors, unless firmly dissuaded, it may try to fulfil the place of a lapdog, getting as close as possible to the person who "belongs" to it.

Wirehaired Pointers, if not being used as working dogs, have a high exercise requirement that, if not met, may lead the dogs to become somewhat hyper. This is definitely not a suitable choice for small spaces, nor is it a good apartment dog: the pointer needs to be "off-leash" and able to run hard for an hour or two every day. It will happily combine the roles of working dog and pet—and provided that the need for exercise is met, pointers will usually be happy to relax for the rest of the time. Although they are hardy enough to live in a kennel environment, like other pointers, this breed is very sociable and does best in a home setting.

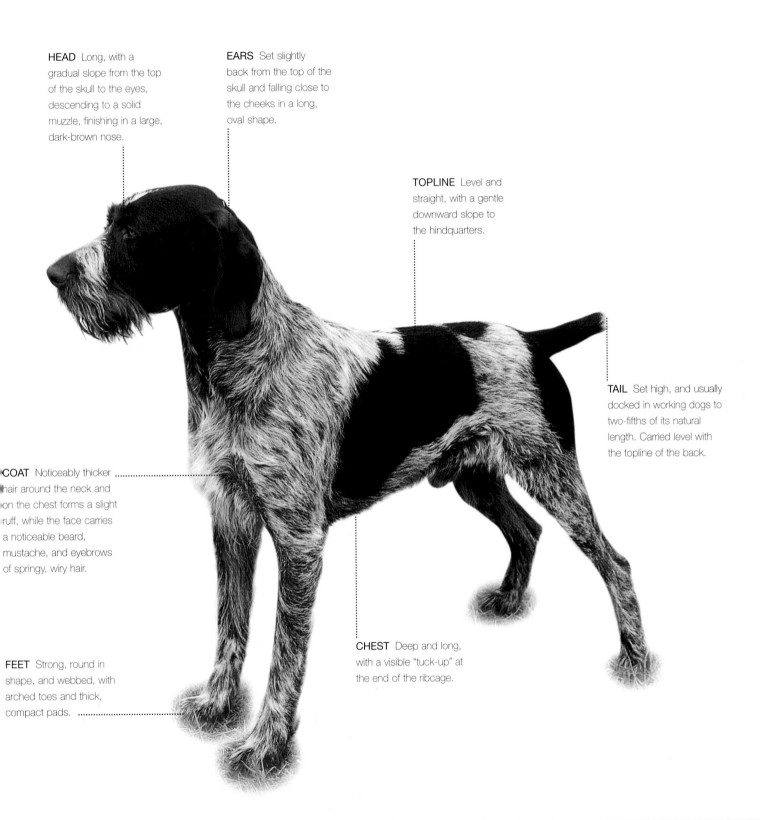

HEAD Long, with a gradual slope from the top of the skull to the eyes, descending to a solid muzzle, finishing in a large, dark-brown nose.

EARS Set slightly back from the top of the skull and falling close to the cheeks in a long, oval shape.

TOPLINE Level and straight, with a gentle downward slope to the hindquarters.

TAIL Set high, and usually docked in working dogs to two-fifths of its natural length. Carried level with the topline of the back.

COAT Noticeably thicker hair around the neck and on the chest forms a slight ruff, while the face carries a noticeable beard, mustache, and eyebrows of springy, wiry hair.

FEET Strong, round in shape, and webbed, with arched toes and thick, compact pads.

CHEST Deep and long, with a visible "tuck-up" at the end of the ribcage.

ESSENTIALS   EXERCISE 🐾 🐾 🐾 🐾   GROOMING 🐾 🐾   EASY TO TRAIN 🐾 🐾   EXPENSIVE TO KEEP 🐾 🐾 🐾

Nova Scotia Duck Tolling Retriever

NOVA SCOTIA DUCK TOLLING RETRIEVER FACTS

SIZE Dog, height at shoulder, 18–21 in (46–54 cm); bitch, height at shoulder, 17–20 in (43–51 cm).

APPEARANCE Small for a retriever; streamlined and compact.

COAT A wavy, water-repellent top layer and a soft, dense undercoat. Shades of gold and copper-red, often with white chest and feet.

BREED HEALTH A breed tendency to hip dysplasia and some potential for eye problems.

AN OWNER NEEDS... Plenty of energy to exercise this lively, intelligent breed. It is good with children and makes an excellent family dog.

Known as the "Toller" for short, this retriever got its name from its unusual method of luring game. Hunters sent the dog out to retrieve a stick or ball from the water's edge. As it played, waterfowl swam over to watch and were shot as they came within range. Today, it is both sporting dog and pet.

HEAD Slightly wedge-shaped skull, only very lightly rounded on top of the head, and tapering to a fine, pointed muzzle.

EYES Almond-shaped, and set quite wide apart, with an intelligent, soft expression that becomes sharply focused when working. Usually golden-brown, but darker or black eyes are not uncommon and are allowed in the breed standard.

BODY Deep and compact chest, with a relatively short body, giving a square, solid outline.

LEGS Well-boned and solid, with medium-sized, strongly webbed feet, enabling the dog to be a powerful swimmer.

ESSENTIALS   EXERCISE 🐾🐾🐾🐾   GROOMING 🐾🐾🐾   EASY TO TRAIN 🐾🐾   EXPENSIVE TO KEEP 🐾🐾

Curly-Coated Retriever

Today, the Curly-Coated Retriever (known as the Curly) is a rarely seen pet, although it is still quite popular as a working dog. It is a very ancient breed, and was first developed in Britain, probably by crossing retrievers with poodle or Irish Water Spaniel Blood. Amenable, lively, a vigilant guard, but with a friendly temperament, quite why this dog has fallen out of favor with pet-owners is a mystery. It is a healthy, usually long-lived breed and, like its popular cousin, the golden retriever, it is good-tempered with children.

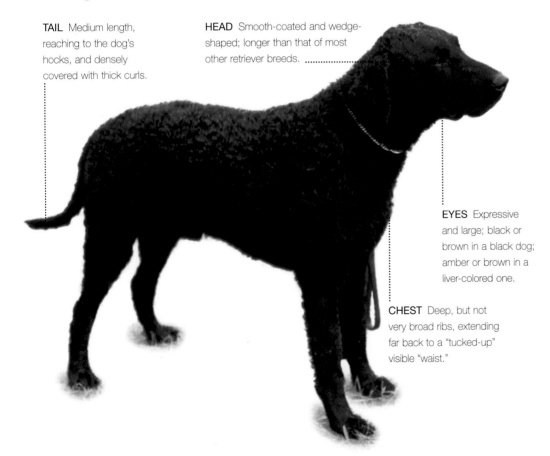

TAIL Medium length, reaching to the dog's hocks, and densely covered with thick curls.

HEAD Smooth-coated and wedge-shaped; longer than that of most other retriever breeds.

EYES Expressive and large; black or brown in a black dog; amber or brown in a liver-colored one.

CHEST Deep, but not very broad ribs, extending far back to a "tucked-up" visible "waist."

CURLY-COATED RETRIEVER FACTS

SIZE Dog, height at shoulder, 25–27 in (63.5–69 cm); bitch, height at shoulder, 23–25 in (58–63.5 cm).

APPEARANCE Very much a retriever in outline, although lighter than some; balanced, robust, and graceful.

COAT The distinguishing feature of the Curly-Coated: a dense mass of small, tight curls all over, except for the face and front lower legs, which are usually smooth. Colors are solid liver or black.

BREED HEALTH Slight susceptibility to skin allergies, eye cataracts, and hip dysplasia.

AN OWNER NEEDS... The patience to seek out this breed, and plenty of energy. This is reputedly an easy dog to train, although its strong guarding tendencies may need to be discouraged.

ESSENTIALS EXERCISE 🐾 🐾 🐾 🐾   GROOMING 🐾 🐾   EASY TO TRAIN 🐾 🐾   EXPENSIVE TO KEEP 🐾 🐾

Hounds

This is a dramatically varied group, from the tall, elegant sighthounds, such as the Afghan Hound, which rely on keen eyesight and an astonishing turn of speed to chase down prey, to scenthounds, such as the Bloodhound and the Otterhound, which are equally reliant on their superlative sense of smell. All hounds, however, will respond well to training. Yet, as is their nature, they tend to become easily distracted if passing by an enticing sight or scent.

Dachshund

DACHSHUND FACTS

🐾 **SIZE** Standard, dog and bitch, height at shoulder, 8 in (20 cm); Miniature, dog and bitch, height at shoulder, 6 in (15 cm).

🐾 **APPEARANCE** Short-legged, long-bodied, muscular, and solid. Despite its small stature, there is nothing fragile about the Dachshund's build or carriage.

🐾 **COAT** Three types: the shorthaired variety has a fine, dense, sleek coat; the longhaired has a soft, mid-length, wavy, coat; and the wirehaired has a double coat, the outer formed of rough, thick hair and the undercoat softer and shorter. Colors can vary, from solid red and cream to the most commonly seen dark browns and blacks, and can be two colors, from brown and tan to brindle, or dappled patterns.

🐾 **BREED HEALTH** For obvious reasons, the Dachshund's back needs special consideration and care. Other susceptibilities in this popular breed include diabetes and some heart faults. Check a breeder's stock carefully.

🐾 **AN OWNER NEEDS...** Time to train: the Dachshund can be independent and very determined. This breed is more energetic than it looks and requires regular walks.

The Dachshund is a small dog, but there is nothing miniature about its personality. Bred in Germany, originally to hunt badgers ("*dachshund*" literally means "badger dog"), the old-fashioned Dachshund was a formidable working breed, famous for its toughness and its stamina. Its bark, deep and throaty, almost qualifying as a bay, serves as a reminder of these origins—nothing could be further from the high, shrill sound produced by some toy breeds.

The original Dachshund was somewhat longer in the leg than the modern version. The latter is available in two types—miniature and standard—but they are identical in everything but size, and even the standard variety still qualifies as a small dog. The charmingly unusual, low-slung appearance of the contemporary Dachshund, however, has come at a cost, giving rise to a number of health concerns. The long back is easily put out, and the breed's propensity to slipped disks and other spinal problems can be the cause of some expensive vet's bills. For this reason, the dogs should not be encouraged to jump, and some owners even carry them up and down stairs. Despite the delicate back, Dachshunds still need plenty of exercise, both walking and playing, to burn off their copious energy. They can be greedy but should not be allowed to become fat, as this can also be a contributory factor in back problems.

True to its origins, the Dachshund is a determined and independent thinker with plenty of attitude; it can prove challenging to train, although many are also playful and will enthusiastically join in if training can be made fun. Although it technically belongs in the hound category, in many ways its personality is more like that of a terrier. Dachshunds are intelligent, but it is not always easy to get them to focus. Some, true to their roots as earth dogs that were bred to go to ground in pursuit of their prey, retain a keen instinct for burrowing and digging.

In grooming terms, this breed is easy to care for; the shorthaired variety rarely needs much grooming, and even the longhaired type is easily kept sleek with regular combing.

EARS Wide, long,, and with rounded ends, and set level with the top of the head. The ear flap acts as a guard to stop grass seeds or other irritants entering the ear canal and causing infection.

EYES Dark brown, sometimes so dark as to appear black, with dark rims. The musculature of the face gives the Dachshund the appearance of having pronounced and expressive "eyebrows."

TOPLINE The line of the Dachshund's back between the shoulders and the hindquarters should be as straight as possible.

TAIL Straight and gently tapered toward the end. Usually carried level with the back or a little lower.

CHEST Broad and with a prominent breastbone. The long ribcage forms a gentle curve as it rises gently to a visible waist.

FORELEGS Short, and with a slightly bowed appearance. The feet are square and solid and may seem to turn a little outward.

ESSENTIALS EXERCISE 🐾🐾🐾 GROOMING 🐾 EASY TO TRAIN 🐾🐾🐾 EXPENSIVE TO KEEP 🐾🐾🐾

Greyhound

GREYHOUND FACTS

SIZE Dog, height at shoulder, 28–30 in (71–76 cm); bitch, height at shoulder, 27–28 in (69–71 cm).

APPEARANCE A fine, elegant outline, sleek, and smoothly muscled. A good Greyhound should look slender and athletic, not bony, or too thin.

COAT A firm, smooth, short coat, in any color or combination of colors. Solid and brindle colors can have white blazes on the face or chest.

BREED HEALTH The Greyhound has inherited few genetic problems. It is susceptible to extremes in temperature, though, and should have a coat in winter and access to shade in the summer. It should also have a soft surface to rest on; its spare frame makes it uncomfortable for the dog to rest on hard surfaces.

AN OWNER NEEDS... To provide a peaceful, calm setting for the dog to relax in. Adopted Greyhounds that have been retired from racing need gentle treatment to settle into domestic surroundings. Most adapt best if it is possible to keep them with another of the same breed. They make good jogging partners for an athletic owner.

One of the most ancient breeds, Greyhounds—or dogs very like them—were being painted on the walls of ancient Egyptian tombs thousands of years ago, and have made regular, very recognizable, appearances in works of art all over the world. Greyhounds are sight hounds; that is, dogs that hunt by means of their exceptionally sharp eyesight and their sheer speed, rather than scent hounds, which use their noses to scent their prey.

The dogs' elegant, elongated outlines are particularly noticeable when seen in motion: a Greyhound at top gallop has a wonderfully smooth and easy movement. Today, the majority of Greyhounds kept as domestic pets are rescue dogs that have been retired from Greyhound racing, which remains a popular sport.

Despite their awe-inspiring speed—Greyhounds are said to be the second-fastest mammal after the cheetah, and can reach speeds of 45 miles (72 km) per hour over short distances—they are not high-maintenance pets. Sprinters rather than long-distance athletes, they need the opportunity to run daily, but do not otherwise need very long walks. They will frequently run hard for a brief time, then amble happily for the rest of the walk before returning home to take a lengthy nap. They are hard-wired to pursue small, running creatures,

though, so when they are not in surroundings where they can run freely, they should be kept on a lead. For obvious reasons, care should also be taken around smaller pets.

Otherwise, the Greyhound's nature at home is gentle, quiet, and affectionate and they readily form strong bonds with their owners and fit cooperatively into a family structure. Racing Greyhounds arrive with new owners already trained, but this breed is easy to train even when raised from a puppy, being naturally tractable and keen to please. These dogs should not be left alone for long periods of time: anxiety is a common Greyhound trait, and it shouldn't be allowed to develop too strongly or it can become a neurosis. They are usually happy in the company of other dogs, however, particularly that of other Greyhounds.

HEAD Narrow and elegant with a long, attenuated muzzle.

EARS Small and held folded back against the head. They move into an erect position when the dog is alert and excited.

TOPLINE Gentle, downward slope from the neck, which is held upright, to the rear. The tail should form a smooth extension from the line of the back.

HINDQUARTERS Powerful and broad, they give the power behind the Greyhound's impressive turn of speed.

NECK Long, solid, and muscular, with a smooth curve into the shoulder of the dog.

TAIL Long and gently tapered, carried low with a slight upward curve or kink at the tip.

| ● **ESSENTIALS** | **EXERCISE** 🐾 🐾 | **GROOMING** 🐾 | **EASY TO TRAIN** 🐾 🐾 | **EXPENSIVE TO KEEP** 🐾 |

Afghan Hound

AFGHAN HOUND FACTS

SIZE Dog, height at shoulder, 26–28 in (66–71 cm); bitch, height at shoulder, 24–26 in (61–66 cm).

APPEARANCE The soulful face and beautiful silky hair disguise a solid, powerful sight hound with elegant lines and a dramatic turn of speed.

COAT Very long and smooth, all over the body, legs, and tail, in any color or combination of colors, although white or colors mixed with white are not favored in the breed standard. Hair is short and smooth on the muzzle and around the eyes.

BREED HEALTH Usually very healthy; some susceptibility to hip dysplasia and cataracts of the eye.

AN OWNER NEEDS... The patience to train this intelligent, self-confident dog, and the funds and time to manage a good deal of grooming.

"Aloof" is the word often chosen to describe this ancient, aristocratic-looking breed. It is believed originally to have been taken from Persia to Afghanistan as a hunting dog; the long coat developed to withstand the harsh, often bitterly cold, conditions of its adopted country. Intelligent and independent, it needs a strong and confident owner to train it to achieve its full potential.

EYES Almond-shaped and set on a slight slant in the head. They are usually black or dark brown, but occasional golden-amber examples exist.

TAIL Heavily fringed and set low on the body, usually with a small curve at the end. When the dog is excited, the tail moves up and is carried high.

EARS Long and set level with the corner of the eye, covered all over with long, silky hair.

BODY Under all the hair, the Afghan has a classic sight hound's body; long-legged, with a high waist and a deep chest.

ESSENTIALS EXERCISE 🐾🐾🐾 · GROOMING 🐾🐾🐾🐾🐾 · EASY TO TRAIN 🐾🐾🐾🐾🐾 · EXPENSIVE TO KEEP 🐾🐾🐾🐾

Irish Wolfhound

Bred, as its name suggests, to kill wolves, this immense dog (the tallest in the world) was in serious danger of dying out when wolves became extinct in Britain at the beginning of the 19th century. It was revived in the 1880s, and today is a popular choice for those with the time and space to dedicate to such a huge breed. Gentle and calm, although somewhat reserved in manner, it usually fits well into family life and gets on with other pets.

IRISH WOLFHOUND FACTS

SIZE Dog, height at shoulder, 34–38 in (86–96.5 cm); Bitch, height at shoulder, 30–36 in (76–91 cm).

APPEARANCE This dog is finely shaped and graceful in movement, although the rather shaggy coat may obscure its outlines.

COAT A harsh, rough texture in a range of colors, from black and gray to red and wheaten. A pure white version also exists.

BREED HEALTH Short-lived (at an average of 6–8 years) and prey to a wide range of inherited problems, including, but not limited to, cancer, bloat, heart disease, seizures, eye diseases, and hip dysplasia.

AN OWNER NEEDS... The space, time and money to cope with training, grooming, and veterinary bills for this giant among dogs.

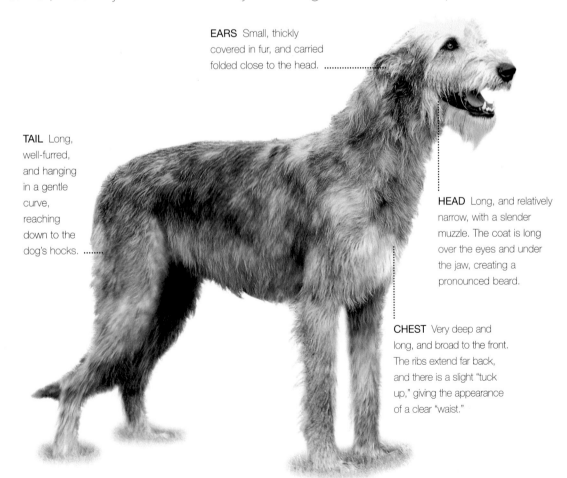

EARS Small, thickly covered in fur, and carried folded close to the head.

TAIL Long, well-furred, and hanging in a gentle curve, reaching down to the dog's hocks.

HEAD Long, and relatively narrow, with a slender muzzle. The coat is long over the eyes and under the jaw, creating a pronounced beard.

CHEST Very deep and long, and broad to the front. The ribs extend far back, and there is a slight "tuck up," giving the appearance of a clear "waist."

ESSENTIALS EXERCISE 🐾🐾🐾 GROOMING 🐾🐾🐾 EASY TO TRAIN 🐾🐾🐾 EXPENSIVE TO KEEP 🐾🐾🐾🐾🐾

Basenji

BASENJI FACTS

SIZE Dog, height at shoulder, 17 in (43 cm); bitch, height at shoulder, 16 in (41 cm).

APPEARANCE Svelte and agile, lightly built for its size. The forehead is often slightly wrinkled, giving the dog a puzzled expression. The tail is set high and tightly curled.

COAT Short, fine, and sleek in a variety of colors, but always with white feet, chest, and tail tip.

BREED HEALTH Generally few problems, but a slight susceptibility to hip and eye conditions.

AN OWNER NEEDS... Patience and an appreciation of the unusual. This dog makes a range of noises from a yodel to a scream, and can be wilful. Although affectionate with their owners, Basenjis don't display much interest in humankind in general.

Originally a hunting dog from Africa, this is one of the most unusual breeds to have gained recent popularity. It does not bark, cleans itself like a cat, and has a self-contained, reserved quality—which can make it challenging to train. Aficionados of the breed enjoy its independent attitude and distinctive looks.

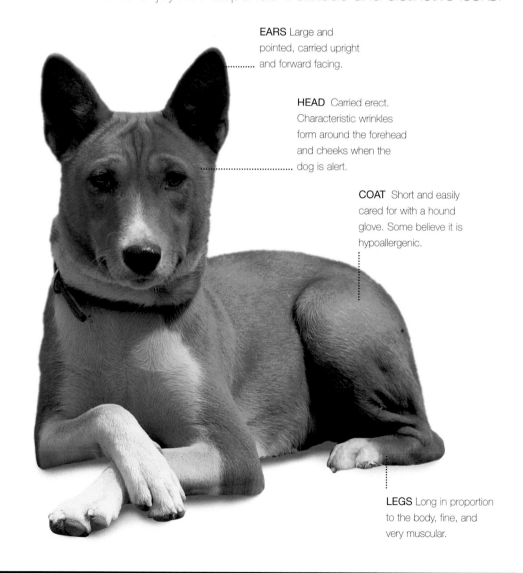

EARS Large and pointed, carried upright and forward facing.

HEAD Carried erect. Characteristic wrinkles form around the forehead and cheeks when the dog is alert.

COAT Short and easily cared for with a hound glove. Some believe it is hypoallergenic.

LEGS Long in proportion to the body, fine, and very muscular.

ESSENTIALS EXERCISE 🐾🐾🐾🐾 GROOMING 🐾 EASY TO TRAIN 🐾🐾🐾🐾 EXPENSIVE TO KEEP 🐾🐾

Whippet

Originally bred in the 19th century for hunting rabbits, and with a top recorded speed of over 40 miles (64 km) per hour, the Whippet can compete with many much larger breeds. Neat, elegant, and undemanding to keep, its main needs are attention from its owner and regular (but not necessarily prolonged) exercise.

HEAD A generous width between the ears, turning to a long, lean, tapered skull with a fine muzzle.

EARS Small, folded ears, known as "rose" ears; held back against the head when resting.

TOPLINE Smooth and flowing with a low, unexaggerated arch toward the hindquarters.

TAIL Long and tapered, carried low with a gentle upward curve in the final quarter.

HINDQUARTERS Muscular and powerful, with a strong backward curve and short hocks.

WHIPPET FACTS

SIZE Dog, height at shoulder, 19–22 in (48–56 cm); bitch, height at shoulder, 18–21in (46–54 cm).

APPEARANCE Compact; fine but workmanlike,with a muscular, symmetrical and balanced look.

COAT Very short and fine, in any color or color combination—the breed standard allows everything from solid black to tri- and parti-color.

BREED HEALTH Whippets are prone to a range of eye problems, but are otherwise generally healthy. They are sensitive to both heat and cold, so pets may need a coat in winter and access to plenty of shade in summer.

AN OWNER NEEDS... To give careful training; Whippets are sensitive. They make good family dogs and can live in a small space provided that their exercise needs are met and they are not left alone for long periods of time.

ESSENTIALS   **EXERCISE** 🐾🐾   **GROOMING** 🐾   **EASY TO TRAIN** 🐾🐾   **EXPENSIVE TO KEEP** 🐾

Basset Hound

BASSET HOUND FACTS

SIZE Dog, height at shoulder, 14–15 in (35.5–38 cm); bitch, height at shoulder, 13–14 in (33–35.5 cm).

APPEARANCE An unusually low-slung hound, with a long, heavy, muscular body, a face with similar characteristics to that of a Bloodhound, and exceptionally long ears.

COAT Short, hard, and weatherproof, in any mixture of two or three hounds, but most commonly seen in black, white and tan, or lemon (pale tan) and white.

BREED HEALTH This dog has a susceptibilitiy to hip dysplasia and knee problems, plus some genetic predisposition to inherited blood disorders, in particular some (treatable) ones in which the blood fails to clot after cuts or injuries. It is important to keep the long, droopy ears clean to avoid ear infections.

AN OWNER NEEDS... The patience to train—the Basset Hound can seem to be slow and resistant to training, although it is intelligent enough to learn. Despite its sedentary appearance, this is a hardy outdoor dog that needs a lot of outdoor activity.

The modern Basset Hound descends from dogs bred in England at the end of the 19th century, the result of a cross between a French breed, the Basset Artésian Normand, and the Bloodhound. The result was a short-legged but very hardy scent hound, the low undercarriage of which allowed it to plunge through dense undergrowth to track its quarry—usually rabbits and hares. Today, it is used for hunting more rarely, but is a popular pet and show dog.

Despite its somewhat ungainly looks, the Basset Hound is a sturdy, untiring tracker that will pursue interesting scents with a single-minded energy. When it is excited, it has a deep, sonorous bark that is more melodic than the high bay of many hounds; also, unlike some other hound breeds, it rarely becomes a recreational barker.

The Basset can easily become distracted by a scent trail and may have a tendency to wander off, so its companion needs to keep an eye on it when it's out walking off the leash. Bred to cope with thick undergrowth, it will not be deterred from making an exploration into even the most densely covered ground.

Personality wise, the Basset Hound is fond of its family and is usually good and patient with children. It can be hard to train, however; although this is far from a stupid breed, even its devotees admit that it takes an unusual amount of time and patience to train because, despite its agreeable and affectionate personality, the Basset Hound simply doesn't seem to understand anyone's motivation other than its own.

When this dog is successfully trained, it is usually by means of food treats. Basset Hounds are extremely enthusiasic about their food, and owners must ensure that they have enough exercise—and that their intake is controlled sufficiently—to avoid the dog piling on weight. Its build is already substantial, and even a moderate degree of excess weight can overstress the dog's joints. Beyond these points, Basset Hounds are relatively easy to care for—regular light grooming with a hound glove and careful cleaning of the enormous ears should keep the coat, and the dog, in good order.

HEAD High, domed skull leading to a long, straight, deep muzzle. The skin is often wrinkled over the brow, and is loose around the jaw and jowls, which gives the dog a mournful expression.

EARS Exceptionally long, large and wide, set quite high on the head and falling well below the chin in loose folds.

PAWS The feet may turn slightly outward at the end of the leg, balancing the width of the chest. They are very strong, large and solid, with thick, round tough pads.

NOSE Large and with wide nostrils, characteristic of scent hounds. The nose is usually black, although a liver nose is permitted in the breed standard.

CHEST A long, deep ribcage, the breastbone protruding slightly ahead of the forelegs. The lowest point of the chest should clear the ground by at least a third of the overall height of the dog, giving enough space for the Basset to move freely and energetically.

LEGS Very short in proportion to the dog's length, but strong and heavily boned, often with wrinkles of loose skin falling around the joints.

● **ESSENTIALS** EXERCISE 🐾🐾🐾🐾 GROOMING 🐾 EASY TO TRAIN 🐾🐾🐾🐾🐾 EXPENSIVE TO KEEP 🐾🐾🐾

Rhodesian Ridgeback

RHODESIAN RIDGEBACK FACTS

SIZE Dog, height at shoulder, 27–29 in (69–73 cm); Bitch, height at shoulder, 24–26 in (61–66 cm).

APPEARANCE Strong, attractive, and athletic, with the unique feature of a distinctive heavily raised ridge of hair running down the spine. .

COAT Short, extremely thick and sleek in feel, in solid shades of pale wheat to deep russet. The breed standard allows a little white on the chest and feet.

BREED HEALTH A strong and genetically very healthy breed, with only a slight tendency to hip dysplasia.

AN OWNER NEEDS... Plenty of time to socialize this large, powerful dog and to give it adequate exercise. Ridgebacks are exceptionally lively in puppyhood, although they usually quieten down in maturity.

Named for the raised ridge of hair running down the center of its back, this large, imposing hunting dog was originally bred in South Africa. It is a good family dog, and makes an excellent guard, but it can be reserved with strangers. These dogs need strong leadership and careful training.

RIDGE There is a visible raised stripe of hair that runs in the opposite direction of the rest of the coat. It starts directly behind the shoulders and continues down the line of the spine to conclude between the hipbones.

TOPLINE A fairly short, muscular neck joins to a very straight and powerful back with only a very slight curve down to the hindquarters.

CHEST The chest is deep, with gently sloping, rather than rounded, sides—indicating plenty of lung capacity, but also streamlining for speed.

HEAD A broad, flat skull, with ears set quite high, which leads down to a deep, powerful muzzle. Eyes may be dark or amber-colored, and are large, round, and set well apart.

FORELEGS Strong shoulders lead down to straight, solidly boned, and muscled forelegs. The feet have arched toes and round, hard pads and are comparatively large.

ESSENTIALS   **EXERCISE** 🐾 🐾 🐾 🐾   **GROOMING** 🐾 🐾   **EASY TO TRAIN** 🐾 🐾 🐾 🐾   **EXPENSIVE TO KEEP** 🐾 🐾 🐾

Beagle

The Beagle has remained unchanged in its essential features for hundreds of years. Cheerful, energetic, and enthusiastic, it was bred as a scent hound to hunt rabbits and hares. It is still widely used for hunting, and is a popular pet, although its naturally noisy expressiveness may need to be discouraged.

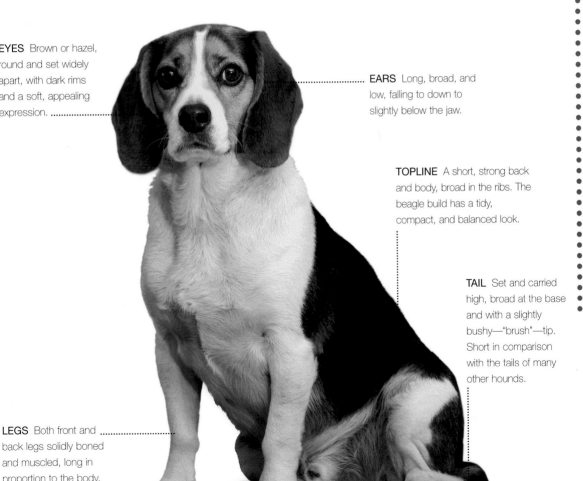

EYES Brown or hazel, round and set widely apart, with dark rims and a soft, appealing expression.

EARS Long, broad, and low, falling to down to slightly below the jaw.

TOPLINE A short, strong back and body, broad in the ribs. The beagle build has a tidy, compact, and balanced look.

TAIL Set and carried high, broad at the base and with a slightly bushy—"brush"—tip. Short in comparison with the tails of many other hounds.

LEGS Both front and back legs solidly boned and muscled, long in proportion to the body.

BEAGLE FACTS

SIZE Dog or bitch, height at shoulder, 13–16 in (33–40 cm).

APPEARANCE Neat, compact, and well-muscled, with long drop ears and a cheerful, energetic demeanour.

COAT A short, smooth coat in bi- and tri-colored mixes of black, brown, tan, and white. Beagles often have a central white stripe down the front of the face with a white "blaze" on the forehead.

BREED HEALTH Generally healthy, although Beagles can be prone to occasional ear and eye infections.

AN OWNER NEEDS... To be prepared to offer this dog plenty of exercise and personal time—Beagles like to be with their owners and make excellent family dogs, with endless energy for play. They are often strongly food-oriented and care may be needed to avoid a pet becoming overweight.

ESSENTIALS   EXERCISE 🐾🐾🐾   GROOMING 🐾   EASY TO TRAIN 🐾🐾🐾   EXPENSIVE TO KEEP 🐾🐾

Bloodhound

BLOODHOUND FACTS

SIZE Dog, height at shoulder, 25–27 in (63.5–69 cm); bitch, height at shoulder, 23–25 in (58–63.5 cm).

APPEARANCE This substantial hound's body is finished wth a heavy, rectangular head, featuring a prominent nose, deep-set eyes, extra-long ears, and an abundance of wrinkling.

COAT Short, thick, and shiny, in black-and-tan and liver-and-tan combinations, or, more rarely, solid red.

BREED HEALTH This is a very strong breed, but it can be prone to bloat and ear infections, and has some susceptibility to hip dysplasia.

AN OWNER NEEDS... Plenty of affection to give this sensitive breed. This dog needs regular and extensive walks. Despite its hefty appearance, it can run very fast.

Bloodhounds are said to have been brought to England by William of Normandy in the 11th century, and the breed has been much valued for hunting ever since on account of its extraordinarily developed sense of smell. While it may not be the most obvious choice for a pet, the Bloodhound fits in well with family life: it is easygoing, affectionate, fond of children, and far more lively and active than its characteristically mournful expression suggests.

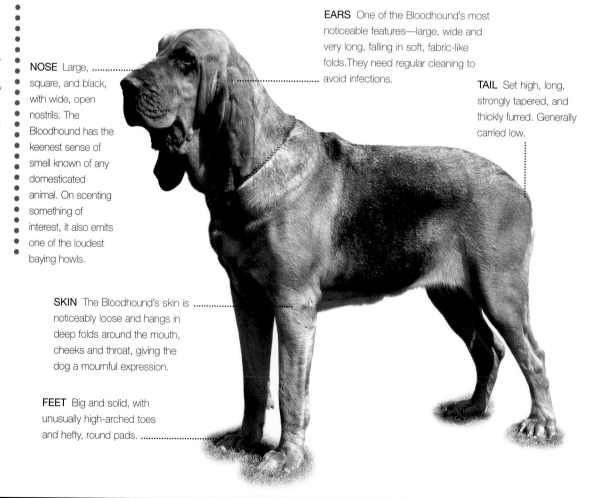

EARS One of the Bloodhound's most noticeable features—large, wide and very long, falling in soft, fabric-like folds. They need regular cleaning to avoid infections.

NOSE Large, square, and black, with wide, open nostrils. The Bloodhound has the keenest sense of smell known of any domesticated animal. On scenting something of interest, it also emits one of the loudest baying howls.

TAIL Set high, long, strongly tapered, and thickly furred. Generally carried low.

SKIN The Bloodhound's skin is noticeably loose and hangs in deep folds around the mouth, cheeks and throat, giving the dog a mournful expression.

FEET Big and solid, with unusually high-arched toes and hefty, round pads.

ESSENTIALS EXERCISE 🐾🐾🐾🐾 GROOMING 🐾🐾🐾 EASY TO TRAIN 🐾🐾🐾 EXPENSIVE TO KEEP 🐾🐾🐾

Otterhound

Large and imposing, this handsome, serious dog is today rather a rarity outside the showring. As its name implies, it was bred to hunt otters in water. It has an extremely strong sense of smell—second only to that of the Bloodhound—and was also a popular scenthound for hunting on land. The Otterhound has a reserved nature, but is intelligent and amenable to training, and is warmly affectionate with its immediate family when kept as a pet.

OTTERHOUND FACTS

SIZE Dog, height at shoulder, 24–27 in (61–69 cm); bitch, height at shoulder, 23–26 in (58–66 cm).

APPEARANCE A strong, square, hound outline.

COAT Dense double coat, with a hard outer- and slightly oily underlayer, in any color or mix of colors.

BREED HEALTH Strong, long-lived, and healthy, but it can occasionally suffer from hip dysplasia and bloat. The breed is subject to inherited blood disorders; if obtaining a puppy, the breeder should be asked about the screening of breed stock.

AN OWNER NEEDS... The space and time to house, train and exercise this large and energetic dog. Its tousled appearance is deceptiive, and the dog needs regular and thorough grooming.

TAIL Thick at the base and well-covered with fur, tapering toward the tip. Carried in a curve, but not so high as to be raised over the hound's back.

EARS Set low on the head, broad, and lengthy, hanging in fabric-like folds.

HEAD Large and long, but narrow rather than square in shape, with deep-set, dark eyes.

CHEST Deep and powerful, with a large ribcage reaching far back toward the loin in an oval shape.

FEET Large, broad paws with a spreading outline and webbed toes to help the dog to swim strongly.

ESSENTIALS EXERCISE 🐾🐾🐾🐾 GROOMING 🐾🐾🐾 EASY TO TRAIN 🐾🐾🐾 EXPENSIVE TO KEEP 🐾🐾🐾

Black and Tan Coonhound

BLACK AND TAN COONHOUND FACTS

SIZE Dog, height at shoulder, 25–27 in (63.5–69 cm) ; bitch, height at shoulder, 23–25 in (58–63.5 cm).

APPEARANCE A sound, athletic, and well-balanced dog, although the legs, while muscular, can look quite fine in relation to the "heft" of the dog's body.

COAT Short, dense, and glossy, a black coat with strongly marked tan "eyebrows," markings around the face, and on the chest and legs.

BREED HEALTH Generally healthy, but there is some risk of hip dysplasia, ear canker and other ear infections, and eye problems.

AN OWNER NEEDS... The energy to exercise this lively dog, and the ability to keep it busy and well occupied, whether hunting or in another capacity such as agility work.

Coonhounds, specifically bred to "tree" raccoons and possums—that is, to chase their prey up trees and keep them there until the hunters arrive—are a numerous group in the United States, although they are less well known elsewhere. The Black and Tan Coonhound is one of the most venerable, well loved by, among others, George Washington and Thomas Jefferson. Friendly, enthusiastic and hardworking, it is still widely bred and used as a working dog and, less frequently, kept as a reliable companion and pet.

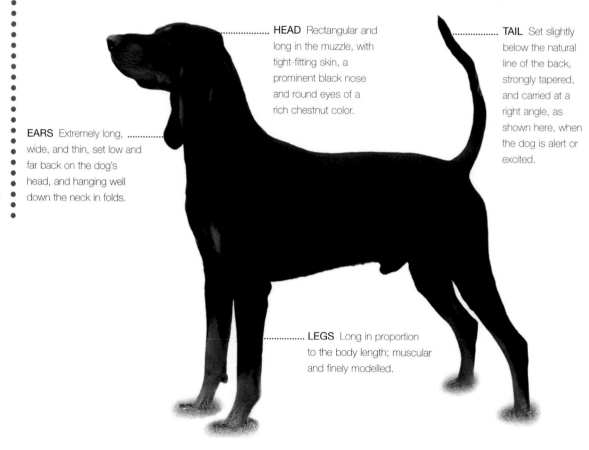

HEAD Rectangular and long in the muzzle, with tight-fitting skin, a prominent black nose and round eyes of a rich chestnut color.

TAIL Set slightly below the natural line of the back, strongly tapered, and carried at a right angle, as shown here, when the dog is alert or excited.

EARS Extremely long, wide, and thin, set low and far back on the dog's head, and hanging well down the neck in folds.

LEGS Long in proportion to the body length; muscular and finely modelled.

ESSENTIALS EXERCISE 🐾🐾🐾🐾 GROOMING 🐾 EASY TO TRAIN 🐾🐾 EXPENSIVE TO KEEP 🐾🐾

Norwegian Elkhound

The sturdy, solid Elkhound is a spitz-type dog, with the curly tail and rather "foxy" face that is characteristic of the group. Bred to bring massive elk to bay and hold them until the hunters arrived, this dog is loyal, playful, and protective, but—as expected from its origins—it is also determined and can be stubborn. This dog should be carefully trained from puppyhood; it can make an excellent playmate for older children, but may be slightly too boisterous for younger ones.

NORWEGIAN ELKHOUND FACTS

SIZE Dog, height at shoulder, 20½ in (52 cm); bitch, height at shoulder, 19½ in (50 cm).

APPEARANCE A balanced, substantial dog with a typical spitz shape, and a keen, alert demeanour.

COAT A thick, hard double coat, with a soft woolly underlayer and a harsh, very straight top layer that stands well away from the body. Exists in shades of gray, ranging from silver to a dark, steel color.

BREED HEALTH Some predisposition to hip dysplasia, liver problems and eye conditions, including progressive retinal atrophy.

AN OWNER NEEDS... Time for training, grooming, plus plenty of exercise. Elkhounds relish the challenge of agility competitions and obedience training.

EARS Large and triangular in shape, placed high on the head, and very mobile.

HEAD Wedge-shaped, with an evenly tapering muzzle and a strong jaw.

TAIL Set high on the back, heavily furred, and carried in a tight curl.

BODY Short and sturdy with a deep, broad chest.

FEET Paws are small comparative to the size of the dog, rounded and compact, with strong, thick pads.

ESSENTIALS EXERCISE 🐾 🐾 🐾 🐾 GROOMING 🐾 🐾 🐾 EASY TO TRAIN 🐾 🐾 🐾 EXPENSIVE TO KEEP 🐾 🐾

Working Dogs

Of course, these aren't the only working dogs—there are plenty of those in the other chapters, too—but to belong to this group, most breeds will have a past that includes heavy guarding, rescuing humans from tricky situations, or jobs that require plenty of stamina, such as sled-pulling. The quality this varied group shares is size—most are big, strong dogs—and all aspects of their personality and care should be carefully considered before you decide to have one as a pet.

Boxer

BOXER FACTS

SIZE Dog, height at shoulder, 23–25 in (58–63.5 cm); bitch, height at shoulder, 21½–23½ in (54.5–57 cm).

APPEARANCE A solid, determined-looking head with a short face and a long-legged, muscular body; it is no suprise that this breed started life as a powerful guard dog.

COAT The coat is short, shiny, and tight-fitting, giving the dog a very sleek appearance. Boxers come in two colorways: tan and brindle. Both may have white markings, but the breed standard dictates that these should not cover more than one third of the body. A pure white variety also exists, but is prone to congenital deafness.

BREED HEALTH Generally strong dogs, Boxers can nonetheless suffer from a range of congenital health problems, including hip dysplasia, diabetes and heart problems. Like some of the other short-nosed breeds, they are also prone to heat exhaustion.

AN OWNER NEEDS... An understanding of the two sides of the Boxer: playful companion and formidable guard-dog. This dog needs lively play and exercise, as well as discipline and training.

This established working breed was created in Germany using early mastiff-type dogs, and first seen at a dog show in Munich in 1895. By the beginning of the 20th century it was being shown in the US, and it was introduced into the UK after the First World War. This strong, lively, and active dog became immediately popular both in a variety of working roles and as a pet, and its popularity in Europe and North America has never really waned since.

Developed to be flexible, the Boxer today is used much more rarely as a working dog, but is still often seen as a companion breed. Despite its unusual and rather pugnacious looks—the short snout and wrinkled forehead can look rather menacing to the uninitiated—the Boxer has a playful, clownish side that is surprising to those unfamiliar with the breed. Powerful and high-spirited, this dog can be very slow to mature, and is also frequently long-lived. Because it may be behaving with the enthusiasm and energy of a puppy up to its third or fourth year, it can prove to be quite difficult to train: boxers are intelligent, but are not always prepared to concentrate on the job in hand—or, at least, the task their owner is trying to teach them. Most are good tempered and can make successful family dogs. However they may be a little too boisterous,

exuberant, and "in your face" to be appropriate playmates for toddlers, although they usually get along with slightly older, respectful children. The dog may also prove a boon to busy parents, as child and Boxer can play happily together for hours.

Usually friendly with people, Boxers are often, although not invariably, combative with other dogs, so canine introductions should be approached with caution. Keep the dogs leashed until the owners are sure they get along.

Generally very healthy, Boxers have one or two weak spots in their hardy makeup: they are not good in extremes of temperature, being vulnerable to heat stroke in high temperatures and chills in very cold weather, and for this reason are best kept as inside dogs—this isn't a good breed for an outside kennel.

HEAD The broad skull and the wide, blunt muzzle recall the Boxer's mastiff heritage and adds to its slightly formidable look.

EYES Large, round, and dark brown in color with dark rims. The Boxer's expression is lively and alert, although the loose, wrinkled skin on the brow can give the dog a rather worried look.

BODY A long, fairly deep chest stretches to a slight waist, while the dog's topline is short, straight, and strong in appearance.

TAIL Until recently, Boxers' tails were docked, as is traditional with working dogs. The natural tail is of medium length, gently tapering from a moderately broad muscular base.

LEGS Both fore- and hindquarters are long and agile. They are moderately muscled and boned, giving the dog an even, balanced look.

PAWS Medium-sized, compact, with noticeably arched toes.

● **ESSENTIALS** EXERCISE 🐾🐾🐾 GROOMING 🐾 EASY TO TRAIN 🐾🐾🐾 EXPENSIVE TO KEEP 🐾🐾🐾

Doberman Pinscher

DOBERMAN PINSCHER FACTS

SIZE Dog, height at shoulder, 26–28 in (66–71 cm); bitch, height at shoulder, 24–26 in (61–66 cm).

APPEARANCE Strong, agile and impressive, with a neat, athletic outline and a constantly alert expression and watchful demeanor.

COAT Short, sleek, and dense. By far the most commonly seen color mixes are black with rust markings, or deep red with rust markings, but much rarer steel-blue or fawn variants also exist, both with the same rust markings.

BREED HEALTH This dog can be susceptible to hip dysplasia, some inherited heart defects and eye problems.

AN OWNER NEEDS... Plenty of experience in owning large dogs, access to generous amounts of space for exercise, the time to train and socialize this powerful breed, plus an awareness of the dog's potential to do damage if not properly controlled. This is not a breed for the novice, or for anyone who is not prepared to spend a large amount of time to its training, exercise, and maintenance.

The Doberman's history is more clear-cut than that of many breeds: it is named for its original breeder, Louis Dobermann, a tax collector in his native Germany in the second half of the 19th century, who combined this role with that of managing the local dog pound. Ideally placed to experiment, when he wanted a tough new guard dog, he decided to create his own. The Doberman Pinscher, which first appeared in the 1880s, was the result.

Elegant and spare in outline, the modern Doberman has not changed significantly from Louis Dobermann's version, except that it is no longer bred to encourage aggression. The result of crosses between the German Pinscher and the Rottweiler, with contributions from the Manchester Terrier and possibly the German Pointer (Greyhound and Weimeraner blood have also been suggested by enthusiasts), it is a large, muscular, athletic dog with a bright, alert, watchful look. Today, it is still widely used as a guard, and its intelligence and trainability have made it popular in a variety of roles, from police dog to guide dog for the blind. A successful show dog, it does well in agility competitions.

It is also a popular pet, although this is a breed that makes quite high demands on an owner. Today, less fierce than its earliest incarnation, this is still a breed that was bred first and foremost as a guard, and it can be aggressive with other dogs and doubtful of, and suspicious toward, strangers. These qualities, combined with its extremely powerful physique, mean that early, careful and consistent training and socialization from a knowledgeable owner are essential to enable the Doberman to realize its potential and to iron out any behavioural glitches long before they become really problematic. Anyone acquiring a puppy should make careful enquiries about the breeding stock before buying.

A properly trained Doberman Pinscher is an excellent and loyal companion, although it is not an appropriate choice for anyone who will be around young children, or who is not themselves fit enough to give this breed the lavish amounts of exercise that it needs.

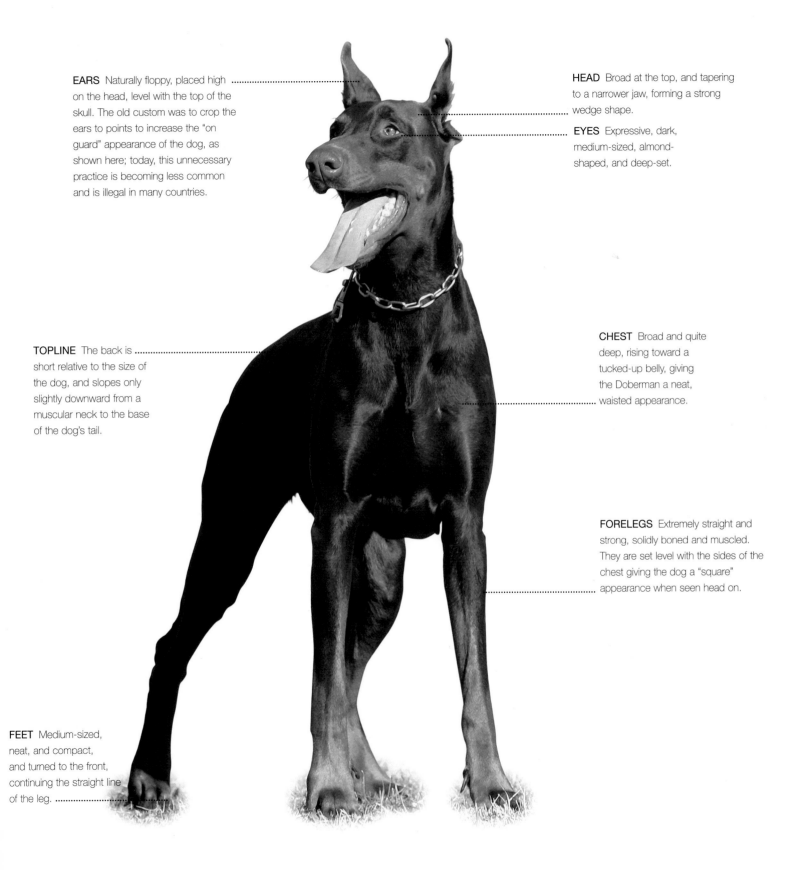

EARS Naturally floppy, placed high on the head, level with the top of the skull. The old custom was to crop the ears to points to increase the "on guard" appearance of the dog, as shown here; today, this unnecessary practice is becoming less common and is illegal in many countries.

HEAD Broad at the top, and tapering to a narrower jaw, forming a strong wedge shape.

EYES Expressive, dark, medium-sized, almond-shaped, and deep-set.

TOPLINE The back is short relative to the size of the dog, and slopes only slightly downward from a muscular neck to the base of the dog's tail.

CHEST Broad and quite deep, rising toward a tucked-up belly, giving the Doberman a neat, waisted appearance.

FORELEGS Extremely straight and strong, solidly boned and muscled. They are set level with the sides of the chest giving the dog a "square" appearance when seen head on.

FEET Medium-sized, neat, and compact, and turned to the front, continuing the straight line of the leg.

ESSENTIALS   EXERCISE 🐾🐾🐾🐾   GROOMING 🐾   EASY TO TRAIN 🐾🐾🐾🐾   EXPENSIVE TO KEEP 🐾🐾🐾

Newfoundland

NEWFOUNDLAND FACTS

SIZE Dog, height at shoulder, 26–28 in (66–71 cm); bitch, height at shoulder, 25–27 in (63.6–69 cm).

APPEARANCE Majestically large and broad, with a heavy coat and a square, noble head, this enormous dog gives an impression of both power and gentleness.

COAT Famous for its swimming abilities, the Newfoundland has an immensely dense, long double coat. The top layer may be straight or wavy, and is waterproof—that is, water rolls off it—and the underlayer is soft and thick. Colors include black, brown, and gray, both solid or with white markings, and the black-and-white mixture known as the "Landseer" after the Victorian artist who often painted this breed.

BREED HEALTH Newfoundlands are susceptible to bloat, hip and elbow dysplasia, and some heart problems. For obvious reasons, they can also overheat in hot temperatures.

AN OWNER NEEDS... The funds and space to be able to keep this enormous dog and the sustained interest to make a lasting relationship with it. "Their" people are very important to Newfoundlands.

There are numerous theories about the remote origins of this immense dog, some more likely than others, but it is known that by the mid-19th century it was working alongside the fishermen in the Newfoundland area of Canada in something like its current form. It helped to pull the nets in and was a renowned lifesaver, with the strength to pull a drowning man to shore, and a waterproof coat that saved it from succumbing to sub-zero temperatures.

Massive but gentle, it seems most likely that the Newfoundland was created out of water retrievers and herding breeds. One school of thought claims it is a remote descendent of the Tibetan Mastiff, to which it bears some resemblance—though how a breed native to the mountains of Asia would have made its way to 19th-century Canada is a mystery. Its working life has not been limited to "fisherman's friend"; it has also been used as a drover's dog and as a draft animal, a role that took advantage of its immense strength.

In character, this breed is one of the steadiest and most loyal of dogs. Calm, unaggressive, patient, and completely devoted to its owner or its family, it acts as a self-appointed guardian and protector of the people around it. Newfoundlands have won many admirers; as well as Landseer, who loved to paint the breed, and who has given his name to the black-and-white variety, the poet Byron was fond of them. His touching memorial to his Newfoundland, Boatswain, remains an accurate tribute to the breed's qualities:

"...One...who possessed Beauty without Vanity,
Strength without Insolence,
Courage without Ferocity,
And all the Virtues of Man without his Vices."

To keep a Newfoundland as a pet requires a big investment of time and money. Although the coat is waterproof—so the dog's love of swimming is not a problem—its grooming needs are still great. Everything about it is on a massive scale, meaning that it is expensive to feed and it needs a lot of physical space. The heavy coat makes it very intolerant of heat. But in terms of temperament and loyalty, fans of this breed would claim that it has very few, if any, equals.

HEAD Huge and broad with a pronounced stop at the start of the muzzle, and intelligent, expressive brown eyes.

EARS Quite small (in proportion with the size of the dog) and triangular, these are set level with the brow ridge and hang straight down alongside the cheeks.

TOPLINE Long and level, with the tail following the natural line of the back. The ribcage is both deep and broad.

TAIL Long and thickly furred, usually carried hanging straight down, sometimes with a slight curve at the end.

FEET Paws are large and round, of the "cat" type, with webbed toes and thick, heavy pads.

● **ESSENTIALS**   **EXERCISE** 🐾 🐾 🐾   **GROOMING** 🐾 🐾 🐾 🐾 🐾   **EASY TO TRAIN** 🐾 🐾   **EXPENSIVE TO KEEP** 🐾 🐾 🐾 🐾 🐾

Great Dane

GREAT DANE FACTS

SIZE Dog, height at shoulder, 33–36 in (84–91 cm); bitch, height at shoulder, 30–33 in (76–84 cm).

APPEARANCE A regal dog, one of the world's tallest, with a graceful, solid build, long legs, and a dignified head with a characteristically gentle, calm expression.

COAT Short, thick, and shiny, in a range of colors, including solid black, steel-gray or fawn, black-and-white (known as "harlequin"), and brindle.

BREED HEALTH Susceptibilities to hip dysplasia, some cancers, and heart problems. Like some other deep-chested dogs, the Great Dane can also be prone to bloat, a serious digestive disorder that calls for urgent veterinary attention.

AN OWNER NEEDS... The energy and the funds to cope with a huge dog. Great Danes are expensive to feed, costly at the vet, and time-consuming to exercise and groom. They need careful training because of their size: an over-enthusiastic Great Dane can unintentionally cause havoc.

Nobody is quite sure where the Great Dane got its current name, as the dog certainly originated in Germany, where it is still known as the *Deutsche Dogge* (*"Dogge"* being German for "mastiff"). Bred from crosses of various types of indigenous mastiff, the two main predecessors of the Dane, the very similar *Ulmer Dogge* and *Danisch Dogge*, were first shown at a Hamburg dog show in 1863, and the breeds were combined under a single name in 1876.

That same year, the Great Dane was announced as Germany's national dog; even the Iron Chancellor, Bismarck, was an enthusiast for this immense Teutonic mascot. Early on in its breed history, it was quite widely used as a working dog, in roles ranging from guard dog to hunting companion. Today, it is mostly kept as a pet.

More than a hundred years later, the Great Dane has not changed very much in appearance since the first Danes were bred for their working roles, but it has become milder in temperament. Today the Dane is generally gentle, friendly, and dignified in manner, although it can still be reserved with strangers and must be discouraged from becoming over-protective of its owners or too territorial in its home. This is not a particularly challenging breed to train: tractable and intelligent,

the main difficulties the dog poses are to do with its sheer size. Potential owners should give careful thought to the very large amount of space even an easy-going Great Dane will take up at home: despite being an appealing dog, it is a serious undertaking as a companion or pet.

Its handsome looks are very distinctive: the head has a noble, solid look, reflecting the mastiff heritage, and the dog's build, quite apart from its impressive scale, is long-limbed and graceful, and particularly beautiful when seen running at speed. Like some of the other outsized breeds, the Great Dane is, sadly, usually quite short-lived, with a lifespan of, on average, around only eight or nine years. And, like everything else about this dog, with increasing age and health problems, its veterinary bills are likely to be large.

EYES Usually dark (although the harlequin variety may have light eyes), medium in size, and deep set, with pronounced musculature above the eye socket, giving the dog noticeable "eyebrows."

HEAD Large and rectangular in shape, and with clear modelling in the face and a square black or blue-black nose.

EARS Medium-sized, and set high on the head, falling forward onto the cheeks with a slight fold.

LEGS Both fore- and hindlegs are quite long in proportion with the dog, with solid bone and muscular development, but not over-heavy.

TAIL Broad at the base, and forming a natural extension to the spine, the tail falls straight when the dog is relaxed, but may curl slightly when it is excited or in motion.

FEET Large and solid with round, thick pads and well-arched toes. In the breed standard, dark nails are desirable and pale ones a fault.

● **ESSENTIALS**   EXERCISE 🐾🐾🐾   GROOMING 🐾🐾   EASY TO TRAIN 🐾🐾   EXPENSIVE TO KEEP 🐾🐾🐾🐾🐾

Akita

AKITA FACTS

SIZE Dog, height at shoulder, 26–28 in (66–71 cm); bitch, height at shoulder, 24–26 in (61–66 cm).

APPEARANCE Solid, alert, and powerful with a large, strong head, triangular in shape and square in the muzzle.

COAT A dense double coat, with a soft underlayer and a thick, straight, harsh topcoat, giving the dog a very furry, bristly appearance. The coat may be any color or mixture of colors.

BREED HEALTH Inherited tendencies to hip dysplasia and problems with the immune system. It cannot cope with extreme heat.

AN OWNER NEEDS... Patience and determination to train this venerable fighting breed to fit into its more modern role as companion dog.

Bred as a fighting dog in its native Japan, the Akita is handsome, powerful, and reserved in personality. Although these days it is often used as a guard dog and as a pet, it needs very careful breeding and training to eliminate any aggressive tendencies. It is not a good choice for a novice dog-owner.

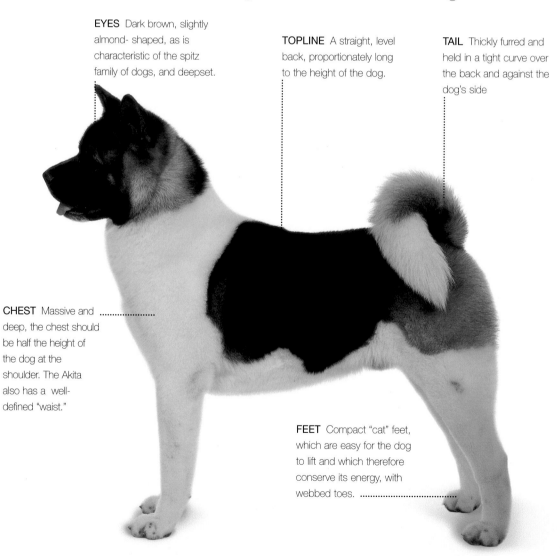

EYES Dark brown, slightly almond- shaped, as is characteristic of the spitz family of dogs, and deepset.

TOPLINE A straight, level back, proportionately long to the height of the dog.

TAIL Thickly furred and held in a tight curve over the back and against the dog's side

CHEST Massive and deep, the chest should be half the height of the dog at the shoulder. The Akita also has a well-defined "waist."

FEET Compact "cat" feet, which are easy for the dog to lift and which therefore conserve its energy, with webbed toes.

ESSENTIALS EXERCISE 🐾 🐾 🐾 GROOMING 🐾 🐾 🐾 EASY TO TRAIN 🐾 🐾 🐾 EXPENSIVE TO KEEP 🐾 🐾 🐾

Siberian Husky

From their roots as tireless sled dogs of great stamina, bred by the Chukchi tribes of Siberia, in modern times, huskies have proved themselves adaptable as companion dogs and pets. They are intelligent, although they may prove challenging to train, and usually have friendly, relaxed personalities, getting along with other dogs and children and fitting happily into a domestic environment, provided that they are given sufficient attention and exercise.

SIBERIAN HUSKY FACTS

SIZE Dog, height at shoulder, 21–23 in (53–58 cm); bitch, height at shoulder, 20–22 in (51–56 cm).

APPEARANCE Handsome, athletic, and graceful and easy in motion, with a friendly, engaged expression.

COAT Huskies have double coats of medium length and in any color. The undercoat is thick and soft. The dog sheds heavily twice a year.

BREED HEALTH Generally very good with no general genetic faults, but extremely susceptible to heat exhaustion because of its heavy fur.

AN OWNER NEEDS Time to dedicate to grooming (this dog is a prodigious shedder) and regular exercise. Provided it gets a good daily walk and enough personal attention, the Husky is easygoing at home.

HEAD Skull slightly rounded on top and tapering down to a medium-length muzzle.

EARS Set high on the head, medium-sized, triangular and carried erect. This puppy is still growing into his ears!

EYES Almond-shaped and set at a slight slant in the face. May be a striking light blue or brown, wall eyes (one of each color) are accepted in the breed standard, and are not unusual.

NOSE According to the breed standard, this must be black in gray, tan or black dogs;liver in copper-coated dogs; and flesh-colored in pure white dogs.

PAWS Oval and medium in size, with round, tough pads and thick furring between the toes.

ESSENTIALS   EXERCISE 🐾 🐾 🐾 🐾   GROOMING 🐾 🐾 🐾 🐾   EASY TO TRAIN 🐾 🐾 🐾 🐾   EXPENSIVE TO KEEP 🐾 🐾 🐾

Samoyed

SAMOYED FACTS

SIZE Dog, height at shoulder, 21–23½ in (53–60 cm); bitch, height at shoulder, 19–21 in (48–53 cm).

APPEARANCE A large, handsome spitz-type dog with a lavish, pale coat, a balanced build and a thickly furred, curly tail.

COAT A very thick double coat, the underlayer soft, thick, and close to the skin, the outer layer dense, straight, and standing out from the dog. The usual color is pure white or pale cream, although a solid biscuit shade also exists, and some white dogs have biscuit markings.

BREED HEALTH Generally good, although there is some predisposition to eye problems and hip dysplasia. Samoyeds can also suffer from a breed-specific problem called hereditary glomerulopathy, a very serious kidney disease. Affected stock should not be bred from, and owners seeking a puppy should check that their breeder's stock is free from the problem.

AN OWNER NEEDS... To be fit and active enough to give this dog the large amounts of exercise it needs, with sufficient time for training and grooming.

Named for the Samoyede tribes of Siberia, who used them as their principle working breed, the Samoyed is one of a number of large, tough, spitz-type working dogs originating from the far north. It is an exceptionally beautiful dog with a glamorous white coat and a handsome, inquisitive face. Bred to do everything from pulling sleds to herding reindeer, the breed was first brought to Britain in 1889, and soon found favor as show dog and a pet.

Samoyeds were popular sled dogs on many polar expeditions, although the breed is not as tough as some other single-purpose dogs bred purely for the purpose. As a multi-tasker in its home country, the Samoyed (somewhat unusually for a working dog) lived alongside its family and even slept with them at night, when its warm coat was especially valued in sub-zero temperatures. It is believed to be one of the oldest of all dog breeds, tests having established that it has not changed in its essentials for nearly three thousand years.

It hasn't gained the sort of overwhelming popularity that can be damaging to a breed, but the Samoyed has always had a stalwart group of followers; its owners' and enthusiasts' association was one of the first breed clubs to be founded in the UK. These dogs have a number of rather idiosyncratic qualities—unusually, they have almost no odor and are thus popular with owners who don't like a prounounced "doggy" smell. They are also fastidious—almost catlike—about grooming themselves. The coat sheds heavily twice a year, and at these times a pet Samoyed is likely to need professional grooming. Another—endearing—feature of this dog is the "smile" it appears to wear whenever it is relaxed, giving it an extremely human expression. Samoyeds are good and friendly family dogs, equable with children, lively, and playful. They do not always mix well with other pets, although this may vary dog to dog. They are not effective guard dogs, being too friendly and outgoing to be good at sounding an alarm for strangers. This is a dog with high exercise needs, so is an appropriate choice for the young and fit. In cooler climates, it can be an enthusiastic jogging companion.

EARS Medium-sized pointed ears, held very upright and placed somewhat at the outer edges of the head. Lavishly lined with fur, both inside and out.

EYES Cheerful and lively in expression, dark and strongly almond-shaped, set quite deeply and with dark rims.

BUILD The luxurious coat, usually with a deep ruff around the neck and chest area, disguises the build, which is that of a fit dog, solidly built but still capable of great agility and speed of motion.

HEAD A deep, gently tapering wedge shape. The nose is usually black but may be a lighter brown or liver-colored. The mouth turns up slightly, which, with the clearly visible black rim to the lips, gives the dog its highly characteristic "smile."

TAIL Very thickly plumed and carried in a strong curve over the back. When the dog is relaxed, it sometimes falls straight down.

FEET Large, long, and with the middle two toes longer than the others—a hare-style foot. Thick, strong pads with a dense growth of hair between them, giving the dog very strong and weatherproof feet.

ESSENTIALS   EXERCISE 🐾 🐾 🐾 🐾   GROOMING 🐾 🐾 🐾   EASY TO TRAIN 🐾 🐾 🐾 🐾   EXPENSIVE TO KEEP 🐾 🐾 🐾 🐾

Rottweiler

ROTTWEILER FACTS

SIZE Dog, height at shoulder, 24–27 in (61–69 cm); bitch, height at shoulder, 22–25 in (56–69 cm).

APPEARANCE A short-coated very robust and powerful dog with a large rectangular head and a solid and muscular build.

COAT A tight double coat, the top layer lying flat, the undercoat relatively light and sometimes carried only on the neck and upper legs. The coloring is a solid black ground with rust or deeper mahogany markings on the head, lower legs, and the inner rear legs.

BREED HEALTH Rottweilers are generally strong and healthy, but there are some tendencies to hip and elbow dysplasia, bloat, and eye conditions, including entropion, a painful problem in which the eyelid turns inward against the eyeball. Poorly bred Rottweilers can have aggression problems. Always obtain a Rottweiler from a reputable and careful breeder.

AN OWNER NEEDS...

The experience, time, and determination to train this masterful breed thoroughly and carefully, plus the taste for providing plenty of exercise.

The Rottweiler hails from Rottweil, near to the Black Forest in southwest Germany. Its original full name was the Rottweiler Metzgerhund—literally, the "butcher's dog"—because, among other working duties, this large, strong dog was traditionally used to pull the cart that delivered the meat. The Rottweiler was also used as a guard and for herding. Its remote origins are unknown, but in its current form it dates back at least 150 years, and possibly more.

During the First World War this breed earned its stripes working as an army and a police dog, and became known outside Germany. It was first recognized by the American Kennel Club in 1935, but was slow to become popular in the UK, where it was only finally registered with the Kennel Club in 1965. It is still widely used as a guard and police dog and has also become a popular pet.

The Rottweiler is an attractive option to dog owners because of its undoubted loyalty, its value as a home guardian, and its strong and attractive looks. This has been a mixed blessing to the breed, because it is an extremely demanding dog to keep successfully as a pet. Rottweilers are highly intelligent and need large amounts of regular exercise; in addition, they are strongly territorial and, unless a Rottweiler is very carefully and thoroughly trained by someone who has a lot of experience with large dogs, its guarding and territorial impulses, allied with its strength, can make it a dangerous dog to have at home. It is not a breed to be considered by novice dog owners, by inexperienced trainers and, above all, by anyone who simply wants to look tough.

If, however, you can fulfil the Rottweiler's needs for careful socialization and training, starting in early puppyhood and continuing all through its adult life, it makes a wonderful pet. It is good with children (although it should never be left unsupervised with them), playful, and enthusiastic around people it knows, and cautious, but not unfriendly with those it doesn't. Its good qualities far outweigh its bad ones—but only when it is carefully raised in an appropriate environment by an experienced, kind owner who knows what he or she has taken on.

EYES Dark brown, almond-shaped, medium-sized, and not too deep set.

HEAD Square and strong, broad between the ears, with a gently arched top to the skull. Coat is tight-fitting all over the head, although the forehead may show deep wrinkles when the dog is alert.

EARS Triangular and set level with the top of the skull, hanging close to the cheeks when the Rottweiler is relaxed, but raising at the base when it is excited. They then appear to extend the breadth of the head.

TOPLINE Straight and level with a very slight downward slope over the hindquarters. Even in motion, this dog gives a square, solid impression.

TAIL Traditionally docked, although this is now illegal in the UK and much of Europe. It is broad at the base with a slight taper and, undocked, is of medium length. It is usually carried low, and never above the topline, even when the dog is in running.

FEET Large and very strong, with a rounded shape, a moderate arch to the toes, and dense, thick pads.

ESSENTIALS EXERCISE 🐾🐾🐾 GROOMING 🐾 EASY TO TRAIN 🐾🐾🐾 EXPENSIVE TO KEEP 🐾🐾🐾

Giant Schnauzer

GIANT SCHNAUZER FACTS

SIZE Dog, height at shoulder, 25½–27½ in (65–70 cm); bitch, height at shoulder, 23½–25½ in (60–65 cm).

APPEARANCE A very large, strong, and solid working dog sporting the characteristic heavy schnauzer beard and mustache.

COAT A double coat, hard, wiry, and very thick outside with a soft layer underneath. Colors are solid black or "pepper and salt"—the latter consists of banded black and white hairs that appear grizzled from a distance.

BREED HEALTH This breed can suffer from a variety of inherited health problems, including hip and joint diseases and eye problems. Breeding stock should be carefully checked.

AN OWNER NEEDS... Plenty of space, plus the time and patience to train and socialize this outsize breed.

Originally developed near Munich in Bavaria as a drover's dog, the Giant Schnauzer is the largest of the three Schnauzer types, but has similar looks to the others—in a much larger package. After its role became redundant, it was used for a time as a guard dog, but today it is mostly kept as a pet or show dog. It becomes attached to its owner, but can be reserved with outsiders.

HEAD Long and rectangular in profile, with prominent beard and eyebrows, and medium-sized ears folded over in a "V" shape.

BACK Very muscular and solid, with a deep ribcage and a straight topline from the base of a well-arched and solid neck.

TAIL When left to grow naturally, strong and of medium length. Until recently, docked short to the second or third joint, although this practice is now dying out.

LEGS Solidly boned, long and strong, both fore- and hindlegs appear straight when the dog is seen full-on from the front or back. Feet are "cat-type," compact, with well-arched toes and dark nails.

ESSENTIALS EXERCISE 🐾🐾🐾🐾 GROOMING 🐾🐾🐾 EASY TO TRAIN 🐾🐾 EXPENSIVE TO KEEP 🐾🐾🐾🐾

Bernese Mountain Dog

This dog originated in the Swiss canton of Berne and was used as a flock guardian and in harness (traditionally, it pulled milk carts) in its home country. As a pet, it is calm and affectionate, although its sensitive temperament means that it must be trained and socialized with care, and always handled gently.

EYES Medium-sized, oval, and dark brown, with an attentive, serious expression.

HEAD Very handsome, broad at the top and with a strong and straight muzzle. The nose is large, square and black.

CHEST Deep and quite broad, reaching as low as the dog's elbows at its lowest point.

EARS Set high, level with the flat top of the head, and of medium size and length, falling close to the dog's cheeks.

TAIL Full and bushy; carried low when the dog is at rest, and no higher than the topline of the body when it is in motion.

LEGS Strong and solidly boned, both fore- and hindlegs are quite straight. The feet of the Bernese are large, with firm, closely-set pads and well-arched toes.

BERNESE MOUNTAIN DOG FACTS

SIZE Dog, height at shoulder, 25–27½ in (63.5–70 cm); bitch, height at shoulder, 23–26 in (58–66 cm).

APPEARANCE A large working dog with a solid, but not a heavy build.

COAT Thick, long, and shiny; straight or slightly wavy. The black ground has a white bib, face stripe and paws, and small rust accents.

BREED HEALTH This is a short-lived dog with an average lifespan of only 7–8 years, and a long list of genetic problems—so it is essential that puppies are only purchased from a careful and reputable breeder. Bernese are particularly vulnerable to cancer, epilepsy, and joint problems.

AN OWNER NEEDS... To invest the time necessary on calm, consistent training, and to be prepared to face possibly high veterinary bills.

ESSENTIALS   EXERCISE 🐾 🐾 🐾 🐾   GROOMING 🐾 🐾 🐾   EASY TO TRAIN 🐾 🐾 🐾 🐾   EXPENSIVE TO KEEP 🐾 🐾 🐾 🐾 🐾

Great Pyrenees

GREAT PYRENEES FACTS

SIZE Dog, height at shoulder, 27–32 in (69–81 cm); bitch, height at shoulder, 25–29 in (63.5–74 cm).

APPEARANCE Strongly resembling the Newfoundland, this breed is distinguished by its paler color and less massive head. It is a powerful dog, strong, and well-built with an intelligent expression.

COAT A flat, long, weatherproof outer layer over a short, woolly underlayer. There is a ruff of fur around the neck. The coat is white, sometimes with markings of tan, gray, or black.

BREED HEALTH Some tendency to hip dysplasia, loose knees, and skeletal problems.

AN OWNER NEEDS ... The money, space, and time to train, groom, exercise, and appreciate this majestic and appealing but demanding breed.

Kept as a guardian to the sheep flocks in the Pyrenean mountain range for many years, this powerful dog was expected to repel all threats, including sheep rustlers and wolves. Still sometimes used as a herding dog, it is also now commonly seen in the show ring and kept as a pet by those with the means to give it the space, both indoors and out, that it needs. The Great Pyrenees is quiet and contained but usually devoted to its immediate family.

TAIL Heavily plumed and carried high over the back when the dog is alert. At rest, it falls in a straight line with a small hook at the end.

HEAD Large but refined; a broad wedge shape, with dark-brown eyes set at a slant, and black nose and lips.

CHEST A moderately deep ribcage reaches down as far as the dog's elbows; the front of the chest is broad and strong.

HIND LEGS A peculiarity of the breed is the unusual "double dew" claws on the back legs. These have no obvious function.

ESSENTIALS EXERCISE 🐾🐾🐾 GROOMING 🐾🐾🐾🐾🐾 EASY TO TRAIN 🐾🐾🐾 EXPENSIVE TO KEEP 🐾🐾🐾🐾🐾

Portuguese Water Dog

This dog's unusual clip (similar to show poodles) disguises its nature: that of an energetic, solid, well-built, and intelligent working dog. It was originally bred by fishermen along the Portuguese coast to help haul in nets, guard boats, and act as a messenger between boat and shore. Today, this breed makes a lively pet—it is naturally keen on swimming—and is successful in the show ring.

TAIL Set quite low, strong, and wide at the base and tapering toward the tip, covered with the same heavy coat as the rest of the body. It is used as both oar and rudder when the dog is swimming.

HEAD A substantial shape, very broad at the top and tapering slightly to a squared, solid muzzle.

EYES Medium-sized and set at a slight angle in the head. They can be black or brown, depending on the coat color.

TOPLINE Straight and level, emphasizing this dog's agile, vigorous outline.

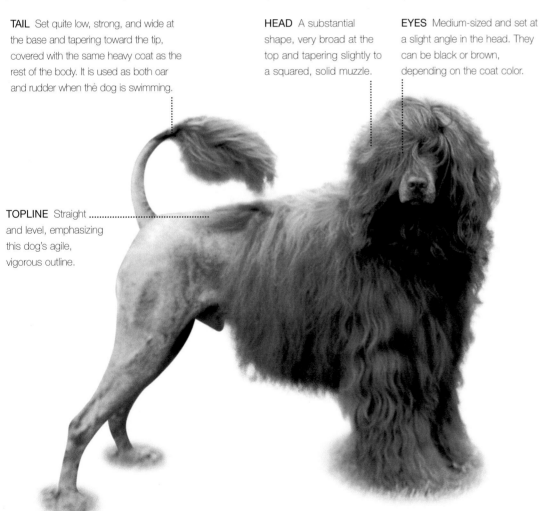

PORTUGUESE WATER DOG FACTS

SIZE Dog, height at shoulder, 20–23 in (51–58 cm); bitch, height at shoulder, 17–21 in (43–53 cm).

APPEARANCE A sturdy, well-built dog with a profuse coat, giving the impression of fitness and balance.

COAT The lavishly thick single-layered coat may be either curly or gently wavy. It covers the dog completely, and comes in a variety of colors, including solid black, white and brown, and black or brown with white markings.

BREED HEALTH Strong and largely free from genetic problems. There is some tendency towards hip dysplasia and cataracts.

AN OWNER NEEDS... Time to spend time with this sociable breed, and the ability to offer swimming as a part of its extensive exercise schedule.

ESSENTIALS   EXERCISE 🐾🐾🐾   GROOMING 🐾🐾🐾🐾   EASY TO TRAIN 🐾🐾🐾   EXPENSIVE TO KEEP 🐾🐾🐾

Terriers

Despite their wide variety of looks, one characteristic that terriers tend to share is personality. Most people either love or loathe these fearless, combative dogs, and as an owner it's good to know what you're letting yourself in for before you buy one. From the large Airedale down to the feisty West Highland, these are amusing, intelligent, and challenging dogs that can offer plenty of fun along with a few disciplinary headaches.

West Highland White Terrier

WEST HIGHLAND WHITE TERRIER FACTS

SIZE Dog, height at shoulder, 11 in (28 cm); bitch, height at shoulder, 10 in (25 cm).

APPEARANCE Small and square with a confident, active bearing. The immediate impression that West Highlands give of being curious and "into everything" is born out by their behavior.

COAT The coat is dense and double: a hard top layer of a medium length is supported by a short, soft, fluffy undercoat. The color is pure white, without colored markings.

BREED HEALTH The West Highland is subject to a high number of inherited conditions, so you should check the breed stock carefully if you are buying a puppy. Problems include a higher-than-usual susceptibility to skin disorders and allergies, and some predisposition to hip dysplasia, ear problems, and diabetes.

AN OWNER NEEDS... To be willing to give this dog plenty of attention, as well as the exercise and stimulation it needs. Westies like to have a good deal of contact with their owners and suffer badly if they are ignored or left frequently on their own.

The West Highland White Terrier, or "Westie" is the original "big dog in a small package." The only small thing about it is its size—its bounce, confidence, and self-belief all belong to a much larger dog. Historically, white terriers were not widely esteemed—their color made it hard for them to camouflage themselves from their prey when out hunting with their owners—so the West Highland was unusual when, in the late 1800s, its color was deliberately bred in.

The—possibly apocryphal—story is that a Colonel Malcolm, a shooting man who lived in Argyll in the west of Scotland, used to hunt foxes with a pack of Cairn Terriers but that one day, misled by the dog's russet color, he shot one of his favorite terriers, having mistaken it for a fox. Upset by his error, he started to breed the white color deliberately into his terriers to ensure that the same accident would never happen again. Whether or not this story is true, pictures exist of the Colonel with some pale-colored dogs that look very much like the Westie we know today.

The West Highland's rather bumptious attitude adds much to the charm of this very popular breed. The game, ready-for-anything approach that made this dog an effective working terrier also ensures that it's an engaging pet that fits easily into most households—although it can be aggressive towards other dogs and needs to be introduced carefully if it is being added to a dog-owning home. One of the most amusing aspects of the Westie is that it clearly has no idea of its size: this means that, on the plus side, you will get endless entertainment from watching it confidently working out the advantages of any position it happens to find itself in. The downside, however, is that you may find it hard to stop this dog from wading in "over its head."

Westies need to be kept busy to ensure that they stay out of mischief. The breed is generally quite noisy, and this dog will need careful training to stop it from turning into a recreational barker.

EYES Almond-shaped and medium-sized, they peer out at the world from under heavy, white eyebrows. This dog has an extremely characteristic gaze—very intelliegent, and full of life and energy.

NOSE Square, black, and large in proportion to the dog. West Highlands also have black skin around their lips and muzzles, and occasionally darker skin around the eye area.

EARS Small and set at the edge of the broad skull. Triangular, upright, and forward-facing.

TAIL Short and thick (the breed standard describes it as "shaped like a carrot!") and carried cheerfully upright in a straight line.

GAIT In keeping with its character, the West Highland has a free, slightly bouncy gait, with the front leg extending a long way forward with each stride.

FEET The forepaws are larger than the hind ones, with big, thick pads, and turn out slightly. The hind paws should face straight toward the front of the dog.

● **ESSENTIALS** EXERCISE 🐾🐾🐾 GROOMING 🐾🐾🐾🐾 EASY TO TRAIN 🐾🐾🐾 EXPENSIVE TO KEEP 🐾🐾🐾

 Airedale Terrier

AIREDALE TERRIER FACTS

SIZE Dog, height at shoulder, 23–24 in (58–61 cm); bitch, height at shoulder, 22–23 in (56–58 cm).

APPEARANCE Tall, long-legged, and handsome, with an elongated, rectangular head and a lavish mustache and beard—key features of the breed.

COAT Hard and wiry, slightly wavy in some dogs, but straight in others. The undercoat is soft but unusually short. The color is a mid-tan all over, except for a lengthy saddle-shape of black or dark gray, extending up the neck and along the upper side of the tail. There is sometimes a white blaze on the chest.

BREED HEALTH Airedales are among the hardiest of terriers, but the breed has some tendency to skin problems and hip dysplasia.

AN OWNER NEEDS...
A taste for energetic exercise, and plenty of time to spend on training—Airedales are smart, but have the strong, independent approach typical of many terriers.

Named after the valley of Aire in Yorkshire, this large, strong dog was originally bred to hunt otters, and proved adept at dealing with waterfowl and badgers, too. It is believed to have been created in the mid-19th century by crossing the Otterhound with one or more types of working terrier, and was first shown in the 1880s, although it was variously also known as the Bingley Terrier and the Waterside Terrier before enthusiasts finally settled on its current name.

The introduction of hound blood resulted in the Airedale becoming the largest of the terrier group, and the dog has been widely used to do a variety of jobs. Before the ubiquitous appearance of the German Shepherd, it was often trained as a police dog; it was also used both as a messenger and as a search-and-rescue dog during the First World War, and proved particularly skilled at locating wounded men for the ambulance crews.

In the 1930s, the Airedale became a highly fashionable breed, and this led to it being kept much more widely as a pet rather than purely as a working dog. It began to be bred for appearance, the focus being on its handsome looks rather than utility. Since that time, it has become less common as a companion dog, partly because it makes high demands on its owner and is not a suitable breed for anyone who is away from home much, or who leads anything other than a highly active life. The Airedale is tireless and intelligent, and it needs to be kept occupied, preferably with athletic outdoor pursuits. It is an excellent choice for someone with extremely high energy levels who wants a dog as a dedicated playmate or an exercise companion. Airedales love to run and, unlike many terriers, they also love water (harking back to their original otter-hunting function). However, without enough occupation for both body and mind, they can become destructive, digging, chewing, and barking relentlessly.

These dogs are not difficult to train, but they are slow to mature, so the training process may go on until their second birthday or beyond. A well-trained and carefully socialized Airedale is worth the effort: owners are rewarded with an enthusiastic, devoted, and intelligent pet.

EARS Moderately sized and placed somewhat to the side of the head, falling forwards in a neat "V" shape from just above the topline of the skull. ·······

EYES Dark and quite small with an ······· intelligent, focused expression characteristic of terriers in general and this breed in particular.

HEAD A long, narrow head, a rectangular shape when seen from the side, and with very heavy fur around the lower cheeks and under the jaw, giving the Airedale the full beard typical of the breed.

CHEST The Airedale's ······· chest is deep but not wide, descending almost as far as the its elbows.

FORELEGS The Airedale's ······· front legs are solid and very straight. The show clip leaves them with a full thickness of fur: originally this was believed to keep the dog's joints warm when it had to spend a long time in freezing water.

FEET The paws have solid, compact pads and dark nails. They are small compared with the overall size of the dog.

ESSENTIALS EXERCISE 🐾 🐾 🐾   GROOMING 🐾 🐾 🐾   EASY TO TRAIN 🐾 🐾 🐾 🐾   EXPENSIVE TO KEEP 🐾 🐾 🐾

Jack Russell (Parson Russell) Terrier

JACK RUSSELL (PARSON RUSSELL) TERRIER FACTS

SIZE Dog, height at shoulder, 13–15 in (33–38cm); bitch, height at shoulder, 12–14 in (30–35cm). (Jack Russells are very variable in size so these, more than with most breeds, are approximate measurements).

APPEARANCE Different specimens may vary widely in build, leg length, and head shape, but the breed standard calls for a balanced, strong appearance fitting to a working terrier.

COAT There are three coat types, smooth, wire, and "broken", which is a mix of the first two. Whichever the type, it is close, thick, and quite short. The colors are white, or white with black, tan, or grizzle markings. Tricolors are a balanced combination of the three.

BREED HEALTH Usually a strong, healthy, and long-lived breed, although there is some predisposition to slipping knee caps and eye problems.

AN OWNER NEEDS... The energy to keep up with the Jack Russell's prodigious stamina, and a sense of humour to help in training this extremely independent-minded dog.

For many terrier fanciers, it is the Jack Russell that sets the standard for both good and bad terrier traits. This little dog has a personality that far, far outstrips its small size. Feisty, energetic, mouthy, fun-loving, and intelligent, Jack Russells may be loved or hated, but they can certainly never be ignored. Some purists insist that this is really a group of types rather than a single breed, because of the extremely diverse appearances of many dogs that represent it.

The original Jack Russell—the man, not the dog named after him—was a hunting parson, or priest, who lived in Devon, in southeast England, in the 1880s (he was also one of the earliest members of the British Kennel Club). He bred Jack Russells using a range of working terriers, with the aim of creating a small dog strong enough to run with the hunt and fearless enough to follow a fox to earth. His dogs became popular with the hunting fraternity, and were soon in demand as lively pets.

Today's Jack Russell has finally achieved Kennel Club recognition, under the name Parson Russell Terrier—it was recognized by the British Kennel Club in 1990, and the American Kennel Club in 2001. The breed standard, though, is still the subject of some discussion, with many dogs that are uncompromisingly regarded as Jack Russells falling outside its relatively narrow requirements in terms of appearance.

Breed standards aside, most Jack Russell's have much in common when it comes to character. They are extremely quick-witted and need firm, cheerful handling and—for their size—a good deal of exercise. They are tough and can be somewhat scrappy with other dogs, although they may also be very playful. Whatever is going on around it, this terrier will want to be in the thick of it. As pets, Jack Russells do best with experienced terrier owners who are realistic about what can, and cannot, be achieved through training, and who will accept this amusing little dog for the character it is.

EARS Drop or semi-drop ears, "V" shaped and forward facing. A wide range of sizes, although the Parson Russell standard specifies that ears should be small.

HEAD Variable in shape (in some dogs the muzzle is considerably more strongly tapered than others) but should be in proportion with the size of the dog. The nose is always black.

EYES Keen and lively, dark, and medium-sized, the eyes are round or almond-shaped (the Parson Russell breed standard specifies the almond shape).

TOPLINE Straight and level from the base of the neck to the hindquarters.

LEGS Strong and quite variable in length; the Parson Russell type is longer in the leg than the shorter, more compact dog shown here.

TAIL Often naturally short, but if not, frequently still docked in working dogs. Broad at the base with a very moderate taper to the tip.

ESSENTIALS EXERCISE 🐾🐾🐾🐾 GROOMING 🐾 EASY TO TRAIN 🐾🐾🐾 EXPENSIVE TO KEEP 🐾

Bull Terrier

BULL TERRIER FACTS

SIZE Dog or bitch, height at shoulder, 18–20 in (46–51 cm).

APPEARANCE A very well-muscled and solid dog, but with a symmetrical and balanced look. Lively and energetic in demeanor, the Bull Terrier should simultaneously convey an impression of both strength and athleticism.

COAT Extremely short, flat, and tight-fitting on the muscular body. The colors most usually seen are pure white (sometimes with a black patch over the eye, or other black head markings) or brindle, although fawn, red, and tricolor variations exist.

BREED HEALTH Generally very strong dogs with few inherited health issues. The white variety occasionally suffers from congenital deafness. Knee weakness and skin allergies are occasional problems.

AN OWNER NEEDS... The time and patience to give this intelligent but sometimes wilful breed firm but affectionate training, and an awareness of the importance of that training, given the Bull Terrier's extreme strength.

Unique in its appearance, the Bull Terrier was developed as a fighting dog in the early 19th century. Its ancestors are believed to include Bulldogs and various types of terrier—some now extinct—but also, more unpredictably, Dalmatians and possibly Greyhounds or Whippets. In the 1850s, an enthusiast named James Hinks took a special interest in the breed and worked on its conformation to produce a dog very like the Bull Terrier of today.

As well as a standard Bull Terrier, a miniature Bull Terrier exists that is identical to its fellow breed in every way except size—it is around 4 in (10 cm) shorter at the shoulder, and less than half the standard's weight. The two types were separated into different breeds in 1939.

The Bull Terrier's looks tend to be either loved or hated: there is no other breed that looks even remotely like it. The Roman nose, the distinctively oval head, and the solid, foursquare body give the dog a powerful look that is a clue to the extraordinary strength that is a key part of the typical Bull Terrier's makeup. Contemporary Bull Terriers are not particularly aggressive: most get along well with people, and many are also friendly toward other dogs—but the healthy respect in which this breed is held comes from the fact that if a Bull Terrier does decide to take action against anyone or anything, this dog is so strong that it can be remarkably hard to dissuade it. It is because of this strength rather than any innate aggressiveness that it is crucial that Bull Terriers are socialized early and thoroughly and responsibly trained; owners need to be certain that, when push comes to shove, the Bull Terrier will do what it is told.

Despite their rather fierce looks, most Bull Terriers are exceptionally playful, and can make excellent companions for older children, although their exuberance combined with their hefty build means that they are unsuitable playmates for toddlers, and they should be discouraged in puppyhood from playing too rough. Their cheerful personalities and enthusiasm for joining in with whatever is going on around them ensure that they fit in well as family pets.

EARS Thin, triangular, and held stiffly upright when the dog is alert. Floppy or "soft" ears are a fault in the breed standard.

HEAD A very unusual oval, or egg, shape, with great breadth at the widest part of the skull, tapering slightly to a strong muzzle.

EYES Small, dark, triangular, and deeply set at a slant, high on the face. The expression is intent and determined, characteristic of the breed.

CHEST Strong and deep, tapering only a little through the ribcage, giving the dog a neat, rectangular outline viewed from the side, with a shallow curve up to the belly.

LEGS The forelegs are very straight and strong, and the hind legs, too, are straight when viewed from behind, giving the overall impression of "a leg at each corner."

FEET Neat, rounded feet with strong pads and well-arched toes. Small in proportion with the overall size of the dog.

ESSENTIALS EXERCISE 🐾🐾 GROOMING 🐾 EASY TO TRAIN 🐾🐾🐾 EXPENSIVE TO KEEP 🐾🐾

Lakeland Terrier

LAKELAND TERRIER FACTS

SIZE Dog, height at shoulder, 14–15 in (35.5–38 cm); bitch, height at shoulder, 13–14 in (33–35.5 cm).

APPEARANCE Looks similar to a small Airedale: a solid, handsome terrier with a characteristic mustache and whiskers.

COAT A double coat with a hard, wiry outer layer in either solid or mixed shades of wheaten, red, black, liver, blue-gray, or grizzle (a mix of red or wheat with black, gray, or liver).

BREED HEALTH Lakelands are a hardy breed, although there are occasional cases of hip-joint problems.

AN OWNER NEEDS... The patience to cope with the feisty terrier temperament and the time to give this little dog quite a lot of regular exercise to keep its effervescent energy to manageable levels.

This terrier was created in the mid-19th century in the Lakeland district of England, both as a ratter and with the specific job of guarding new lambs from foxes. Bedlington, Border, and Dandie Dinmont terriers all went into the mix, probably also with some Fox Terrier blood. The Lakeland, often kept as a pet today, is a busy little dog with plenty of energy and enthusiasm for life. This breed tends to be quite "barky" and are thus good house guards; they also need plenty of exercise and are usually reasonably patient with children.

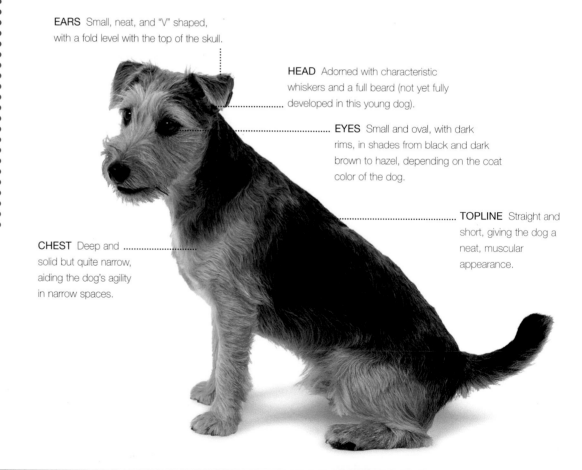

EARS Small, neat, and "V" shaped, with a fold level with the top of the skull.

HEAD Adorned with characteristic whiskers and a full beard (not yet fully developed in this young dog).

EYES Small and oval, with dark rims, in shades from black and dark brown to hazel, depending on the coat color of the dog.

TOPLINE Straight and short, giving the dog a neat, muscular appearance.

CHEST Deep and solid but quite narrow, aiding the dog's agility in narrow spaces.

ESSENTIALS   EXERCISE 🐾 🐾 🐾   GROOMING 🐾 🐾 🐾   EASY TO TRAIN 🐾 🐾 🐾   EXPENSIVE TO KEEP 🐾 🐾

Wirehaired Fox Terrier

Bred as rabbiters, ratters and, as their name would suggest, to follow the hunt and dig out foxes, Fox Terriers, both the wire- and smoothhaired versions, seem likely to have originated from a mixture of the old English Black and Tan terriers, Bull Terriers, and Beagles. This dog has the true terrier personality: strong-minded, full of vitality, and somewhat stubborn to train, it is fiercely loyal to its family and, trained and socialized properly, can be a characterful pet.

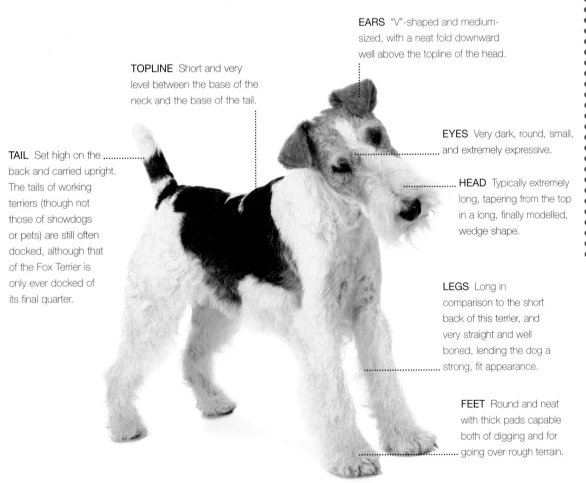

EARS "V"-shaped and medium-sized, with a neat fold downward well above the topline of the head.

TOPLINE Short and very level between the base of the neck and the base of the tail.

EYES Very dark, round, small, and extremely expressive.

TAIL Set high on the back and carried upright. The tails of working terriers (though not those of showdogs or pets) are still often docked, although that of the Fox Terrier is only ever docked of its final quarter.

HEAD Typically extremely long, tapering from the top in a long, finally modelled, wedge shape.

LEGS Long in comparison to the short back of this terrier, and very straight and well boned, lending the dog a strong, fit appearance.

FEET Round and neat with thick pads capable both of digging and for going over rough terrain.

WIREHAIRED FOX TERRIER FACTS

SIZE Dog, height at shoulder, 14–16 in (35.5–40.5 cm); bitch, height at shoulder, 13–15 in (33–38 cm).

APPEARANCE Square set and moderate in build, with a characterful terrier face and medium leg and back length, giving a strong but agile impression.

COAT A very wiry, coarse, tough topcoat overlaying an extremely short, fine underlayer. Colors are either solid white or white with black or tan markings, but with white still predominant.

BREED HEALTH Generally healthy, but Fox Terriers sometimes suffer from skin and eye problems.

AN OWNER NEEDS... Patience and a sense of humor, to train this terrier and cope with its extremely typical terrier personality.

ESSENTIALS EXERCISE 🐾🐾🐾🐾 GROOMING 🐾🐾🐾 EASY TO TRAIN 🐾🐾🐾 EXPENSIVE TO KEEP 🐾🐾

Cairn Terrier

CAIRN TERRIER FACTS

SIZE Dog, height at shoulder, 12 in (30 cm); bitch, height at shoulder, 10–11 in (25–28 cm).

APPEARANCE A squarely built, strong little dog with a keen, alert expression under a natural fringe of shaggy hair.

COAT The coat is double-layered, with a harsh, rough top coat and a short, soft underlayer close to the skin. A wide range of colors is available, including brindle, tan, wheat, cream or red, and all shades of gray, from pale to almost black. Pure black and pure white are not allowed in the breed standard.

BREED HEALTH Tough and hardy, the Cairn Terrier has fewer inherited health problems than many breeds, although cairns can suffer from a range of eye problems, and there is some tendency to hip dysplasia and weaknesses of the knees.

AN OWNER NEEDS...
The determination to train this typically energetic and sometimes wilful terrier, and an enthusiasm for outdoor play and exercise to match the Cairn's own.

One of a large number of Scottish terrier breeds originally developed to hunt vermin—an all-purpose word that can encompass everything from rats and mice to foxes—the Cairn Terrier originated in the west of Scotland, and the strain that provides the backbone of today's stock is traceable back to the Isle of Skye. This shaggy, lively small terrier had become a distinct breed by the mid-19th century and was first shown to a breed standard in 1909.

This terrier's name comes from the Scottish word for a heap of stones, "cairn," and it is the sort of terrain in which the dog would originally have hunted, digging out its prey from stone walls, heaps of boulders or underground burrows with enthusiasm. Today, these qualities remain evident in the modern dog, which is still used as a working terrier but which has also become a popular pet. It played a part in the development of some of the comparatively more recent terrier breeds, among them the West Highland White, Norfolk and Norwich Terriers.

The Cairn's natural appearance is solid and endearingly scruffy; even in the show ring, its groomed style is "natural," and its rough, weatherproof coat does not need lengthy grooming, although regular brushing will help to avoid knots and tangles. Its personality is energetic and tenacious, although it is easier to train than some others in the terrier group. Like all terriers, it demands patience and persistance from its trainer, being an independent thinker that will take its time to see the benefits of training. Obedience training is best accomplished with positive reinforcement.

Today, the Cairn is a popular pet and the breed's adaptability means that it can fit into most surroundings, although it needs enough exercise and mental stimulation to stave off boredom and bring out the best in its feisty personality. Despite its small size, this is not a dog that will be happy to sit around all day.

The Cairn Terrier generally gets along with other dogs if they are carefully introduced, but is liable to chase cats unless raised with them, and cannot be trusted around smaller pets.

EARS Triangular, upright, set well apart on the skull, and forward-facing.

EYES Wide-apart and deep-set, with a merry, alert expression. In shades of brown, from hazel to very dark, depending on the coat color of the dog.

NOSE Black, and large in proportion with the overall size of the dog,

HEAD Broad at the top, tapering slightly toward a strong muzzle. Heavily furred all over except for the ears, with dense eyebrows, mustache, and beard.

TOPLINE Very straight, leading from a well-arched and muscled neck to a thick, strong tail of medium length.

LEGS Forelegs are straight and strong, although the front feet may turn outward slightly.

ESSENTIALS EXERCISE 🐾🐾🐾 GROOMING 🐾🐾🐾 EASY TO TRAIN 🐾🐾🐾 EXPENSIVE TO KEEP 🐾

Scottish Terrier

SCOTTISH TERRIER FACTS

SIZE Dog, height at shoulder, 10–11 in (25–28 cm); bitch, height at shoulder, 9–10 in (23–25 cm).

APPEARANCE Square, compact and solid, with a brisk and very characteristic, swaying gait.

COAT Wiry, thick topcoat over a dense, soft undercoat, usually in black, brindle, or dark gray, but more rarely also wheaten.

BREED HEALTH Strong and usually healthy, this breed has a susceptibility to overactive thyroid and epilepsy and can suffer from a breed-specific condition called Scottie cramp.

AN OWNER NEEDS... Patience and a sense of humor during training, and the capacity to enjoy this breed's self-important confidence.

Confident, strong-minded and reserved, bred to dig out game that had gone to ground, the Scottish Terrier has a number of typical terrier traits, and some that are particularly its own. It is devoted to its immediate family, but can be dour with outsiders, and sometimes unfriendly towards other dogs. Today, it is almost invariably kept as a pet, but retains its prodigious digging ability.

EARS Triangular, forward-facing, and upright, set high on the dog's skull.

HEAD Long and rectangular, with a heavy and distinctive mustache and beard.

NECK Thick and strong, curving smoothly into a short, straight back.

CHEST Very broad and deep, extending downward between the short forelegs.

FEET Large and round, with broad, thick pads and strong nails.

ESSENTIALS EXERCISE 🐾🐾🐾 GROOMING 🐾🐾🐾🐾 EASY TO TRAIN 🐾🐾🐾🐾 EXPENSIVE TO KEEP 🐾🐾🐾

Bedlington Terrier

The unusual looks of the Bedlington are often said to be "lamb-like," but this feisty terrier does not have a peaceful character to match. Bred in the north of England to hunt rats, probably from a mix of terriers and some Whippet blood, the breed was at one time favored by poachers and actually nicknamed "the poacher's dog." Today, it has many enthusiasts for its qualities as a pet.

TAIL Set low, and tapering from a broad base to a narrow tip. Like the greyhound tail, carried low in a shallow curve.

HEAD Long, narrow face with a rounded skull. Eyes can be dark brown or hazel, and are almond-shaped, deep-set and expressive.

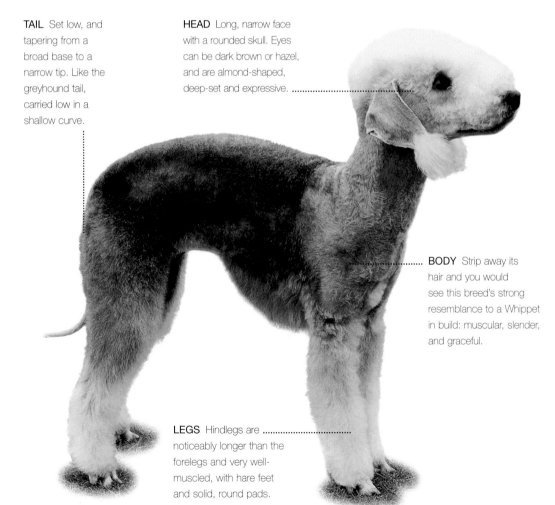

BODY Strip away its hair and you would see this breed's strong resemblance to a Whippet in build: muscular, slender, and graceful.

LEGS Hindlegs are noticeably longer than the forelegs and very well-muscled, with hare feet and solid, round pads.

BEDLINGTON TERRIER FACTS

SIZE Dog, height at shoulder, 16–17½ in (40–44 cm); bitch, height at shoulder, 15–16½ in (38–42 cm).

APPEARANCE An arched back, thick fur on the top of the head and pompom fringes on the ears lend this dog unusual looks, exaggerated by its distinctive show clip.

COAT A single coat of woolly and hard hair mixed, which stands out from the body. The most usual coloring is blue-gray, but there are variations in liver, tan, and sandy fawn.

BREED HEALTH Some susceptibility to inherited eye problems and kidney disease.

AN OWNER NEEDS... The ability to train patiently. Coercion does not work with this terrier, which has a strong streak of stubborness.

ESSENTIALS EXERCISE 🐾 🐾 🐾   GROOMING 🐾 🐾 🐾 🐾   EASY TO TRAIN 🐾 🐾 🐾 🐾   EXPENSIVE TO KEEP 🐾 🐾 🐾 🐾

Glen of Imaal Terrier

GLEN OF IMAAL TERRIER FACTS

SIZE Dog or bitch, height at shoulder, 12½–14 in (32–35.5 cm).

APPEARANCE Low-set and solid, longer than it is tall, with a balanced, active, alert look.

COAT Double-coat of medium length, with a hard topcoat and a soft, silky underlayer. It may come in blue-gray, ranging from a light gray to a deep slate color; in brindle, or a range of shades of wheat, from pale gold to reddish.

BREED HEALTH Generally very strong and healthy, the breed can be prone to progressive retinal atrophy, a disease of the eyes, and to some heart problems.

AN OWNER NEEDS... The patience to hunt out a puppy and the energy to exercise and socialize this lively dog.

This unusual little terrier was originally bred as a working farm dog with a sideline in fox- and badger-hunting, and named for the region in County Wicklow, Ireland, where it originated. Officially registered as a breed in Ireland in the 1930s, it is still comparatively rare outside its native country, where it is kept as a farm dog and a family pet. Sturdy and solid, with a studiedly unkempt look, it is easy to care for and has the reputation of being good with children, very playful, and a little more laid back than many other terrier breeds.

TAIL Medium length and carried high, this dog's tail was invariably docked to around half its length in working dogs, although the practice is dying out today.

BACK Long and straight, very strong and muscular, but still giving a balanced, active appearance.

HEAD Strong and balanced with a broad skull and a solid, squarish muzzle. The face is covered with hair, with pronounced "eyebrows" and a small beard.

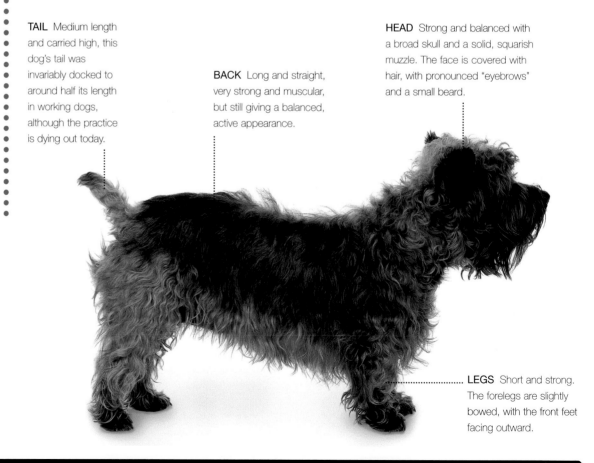

LEGS Short and strong. The forelegs are slightly bowed, with the front feet facing outward.

ESSENTIALS   **EXERCISE**   **GROOMING**   **EASY TO TRAIN**   **EXPENSIVE TO KEEP**

Staffordshire Bull Terrier

In the 18th century, the forebears of the Staffordshire Bull Terrier were bred for fighting, probably by crossing a Bulldog with one or more types of terrier. The result was a medium-sized dog that was tenacious, intelligent and immensely strong. In modern times, the "Staffy" enjoys enormous success as a pet. Famously good with children and affectionate with its owners, the dog may still display its heritage in skirmishes with other canines—and, because this is such a strong breed, it is crucial that it is carefully trained.

STAFFORDSHIRE BULL TERRIER FACTS

SIZE Dog, height at shoulder, 15–16 in (38–41 cm) ; bitch, height at shoulder, 14–15 in (35.5–38 cm).

APPEARANCE Sleek and extremely muscular, with a square, cleanly modelled face that clearly displays the Bulldog in its makeup.

COAT Very short, shiny and tight fitting, in a wide range of colors: red, fawn, black, white, blue-gray, and brindle, or any of these with white.

BREED HEALTH Few inherited conditions or predispositions to problems, but the Staffordshire can suffer from epilepsy and some eye conditions, including cataracts.

AN OWNER NEEDS... The determination and patience to train this strong-minded but friendly dog, and the time to wear out its prodigious energy with walks, games, and exercise.

HEAD Square, broad, and deep with strongly defined muscles in the cheeks and clear modelling on the brow, which is very wide. Short muzzle with a large black nose, and dark, round eyes.

EARS Half-rose (semi-erect) ears, thin, and fine.

BODY Extremely muscular, but well-modelled, broad through the ribs and tapering beyond the ribs to comparatively narrow loins.

TAIL Set and carried quite low, and of medium length, tapering gently to a point.

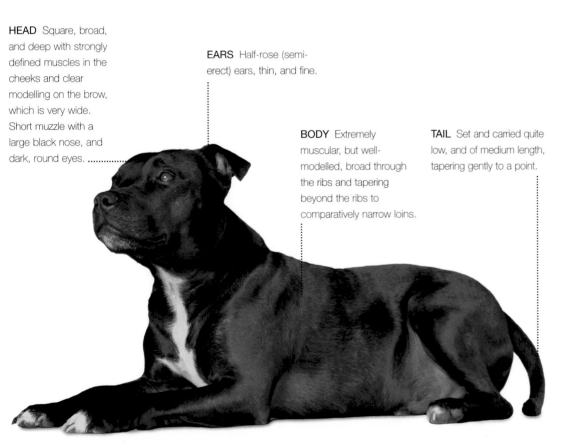

ESSENTIALS   EXERCISE 🐾🐾🐾   GROOMING 🐾   EASY TO TRAIN 🐾🐾🐾   EXPENSIVE TO KEEP 🐾🐾

Border Terrier

BORDER TERRIER FACTS

SIZE Dog or bitch, height at shoulder, 10 in (25 cm).

APPEARANCE Workmanlike and attractive, although not elegant. This dog has a strong, spare build, and is leggy, with the ability to run fast as well as to dig.

COAT A double coat, with a short, wiry topcoat underlaid by a softer, thick underlayer. Colors can be grizzle, wheat, red, tan, or blue (gray). The muzzle and ears should be dark, and white should appear only in a blaze on the chest.

BREED HEALTH Borders are usually healthy; there is some tendency to patellar luxation, a problem with the kneecaps, and a susceptibility to glaucoma and other eye problems.

AN OWNER NEEDS... Moderate time for exercise and training this rather atypically mellow terrier. This breed needs company, and enough walks and games to keep it lively and healthy. It fits in well with family life, but will be equally suited to a single owner.

Although the Border Terrier is perhaps one of the less distinguished of the terrier family in appearance, there is a pleasing utility about its neat build and unexaggerated features. Originally bred to run with the hunt and to dig out foxes that had gone to earth, it needed to be small enough to burrow but long-legged enough and with sufficient stamina to accompany the much larger foxhounds. Today, it is rarely used for hunting, but is an extremely popular pet.

The toughness that was originally bred into this terrier to enable it to do its job is concealed under a deceptively mild persona. As a working terrier, it had an unrelenting reputation, able to pursue a fox and flush it out for the hounds, sometimes after miles of running. It was first heard of as a distinct breed in the middle of the 19th century, raised in the lands around the border between England and Scotland (hence the name, "Border"), and was first recognized, with its own breed standard, in 1920. Since then it has been a successful show dog, and as its working career has dwindled, its role as a pet has increased.

By terrier standards this dog has a relaxed character, and is cheerful, easily trained, easygoing, and largely lacking the "hyper" quality that characterizes many others in the terrier family. It is also—unusually for a terrier—quite keen to please its owners, which makes it relatively easy and quick to train. Nor is it particularly demanding to keep; the short, rough coat seems to shed dirt and a weekly groom with a brush and comb keep it in good condition.

Border Terriers need regular exercise; as might be expected from their background, they are high-energy dogs and, if bored, may create their own amusements. They are keen on digging and can, if neglected, become recreational barkers, so it's a good idea to direct their attention to approved pursuits. This dog can easily be engaged in any family activity and maintains a keen interest in what is going on around it. Most socialized Border Terriers will get along with other dogs—and cats, if they are introduced carefully—although they should not be trusted with small animals that, to them, look like prey.

EARS Medium-sized "V" shaped ears that fall forward.Set at the sides of the head and level with the top of the skull. ....

HEAD The breed standard compares the Border Terrier's head to that of an otter: broad at brow, full-cheeked, and narrowing toward the muzzle.

EYES Round, with dark rims. Usually a light brown or hazel, and with the characteristic keen, alert terrier gaze.

CHEST A deep but also narrow ribcage with a shallow "tuck up" to the loin at the end of the ribs, giving the dog a straight underline.

TAIL Thick at the base, of medium length, and tapering a little toward the end. Carried upright, but straight rather than in a curve.

LEGS Muscular but not too heavy, and long in proportion to the overall size of the dog. Forelegs are straight; paws are small, compact, and rounded with well-arched toes. ....

● **ESSENTIALS**   **EXERCISE** 🐾 🐾   **GROOMING** 🐾   **EASY TO TRAIN** 🐾   **EXPENSIVE TO KEEP** 🐾

Kerry Blue Terrier

KERRY BLUE TERRIER FACTS

SIZE Dog, height at shoulder, 18–19½ in (46–49.5 cm); bitch, height at shoulder,17½–19 in (44.5–48 cm).

APPEARANCE A strong, well-set up terrier with a foursquare appearance and a keen, energetic look. Regular professional grooming is essential to maintain the distinctive Kerry Blue outline.

COAT Very distinctive, thick, silky fur with a slightly "kinky" astrakhan (woolly) texture, in solid blue-gray, darkening to slate, sometimes with a small white patch on the chest.

BREED HEALTH Kerry Blues can suffer from hip dysplasia, and may have some predisposition to disorders of the immune system.

AN OWNER NEEDS... Plenty of determination to train and discipline this independent and very active dog.

This Irish-bred terrier was used as an all-round sports dog in County Kerry, where it hunted otters, as well as foxes, badgers, and rabbits. It is both a strong swimmer and a fast runner—and can be an aggressive fighter if the occasion arises. The Kerry Blue is devoted to its owner, but has its full share of terrrier wilfulness and needs firm, calm handling to bring out the best in it.

HEAD A flat skull leads to a rectangular face with only a gentle tapering toward the muzzle. The Kerry Blue is heavily bearded and mustached.

TOPLINE The long, developed neck slopes to a short back that should continue to a straight line to the tail.

TAIL Carried upright, although in a straight line rather than a curve. Of medium length, slightly tapered, and set high on the back.

LEGS Lavish furring disguises its solid, straight forelegs and extremely muscular hindquarters. In movement, the gait is characteristically loose and very easy.

CHEST The ribcage is very deep but only moderately broad, and the body tucks up sharply beyond it.

ESSENTIALS   EXERCISE 🐾🐾🐾🐾   GROOMING 🐾🐾🐾🐾   EASY TO TRAIN 🐾🐾🐾   EXPENSIVE TO KEEP 🐾🐾🐾🐾

Dandie Dinmont Terrier

Named for a character in *Guy Mannering*, a novel by Sir Walter Scott, this small terrier was bred in the north of England, and used to hunt foxes and badgers. Despite its somewhat whimsical appearance in full show clip—a long, low-slung body finished off with a topknot perched on its head—this is a tough little dog that enjoys energetic exercise and games, and which has a more mellow streak than some of its fellow terriers. Originally kept in packs, it usually gets on with other dogs and is also well-disposed toward children.

DANDIE DINMONT TERRIER FACTS

SIZE Dog, height at shoulder, 9–11 in (23–28 cm); bitch, height at shoulder, 8–10 in (20–25 cm).

APPEARANCE Long and low, Dandie Dinmonts bear a slight resemblance to Dachshunds at first glance, but have more tousled coats and much squarer faces.

COAT An unusual mixture of hard and soft hair, groomed by plucking rather than clipping. The head hair is very silky. The colors are known as "pepper"—shades of black to gray—and "mustard"—red brown to pale fawn.

BREED HEALTH A propensity to hip dysplasia and back problems, including slipped disks.

AN OWNER NEEDS... Time for training and exercise. A loving home where it can happily join in with family life and whatever is going on around it.

TAIL The tail is long and fairly thick, and is carried in a characteristic shallow curve, known as a "scimitar" tail.

HEAD The topknot conceals a strong, large head tapering a little to a strong, square muzzle and a dark nose.

TOPLINE The back has a prounouced dip after the neck, then rises into a straight arch over the loins.

LEGS The legs are short but strong, the hind legs slightly longer than the front ones.

ESSENTIALS   **EXERCISE** 🐾 🐾 🐾   **GROOMING** 🐾 🐾 🐾 🐾   **EASY TO TRAIN** 🐾 🐾 🐾   **EXPENSIVE TO KEEP** 🐾 🐾 🐾

Manchester Terrier

MANCHESTER TERRIER FACTS

SIZE Dog, height at shoulder, 16 in (41 cm); bitch, height at shoulder, 15 in (38 cm).

APPEARANCE Neat and smart in outline, with a slight but muscular build, and a typically keen terrier expression.

COAT Very short, dense, and close-fitting, with a high gloss. The color is black with tan markings, usually on the feet, chest, and face.

BREED HEALTH A very strong and usually long-lived dog, but Von Willebrand's disease, a serious blood-clotting disorder, is comparatively common in this dog, and breeding stock should be checked.

AN OWNER NEEDS... The time to train and socialize this typical terrier. Although independent thinkers, Manchesters are not usually wilful.

Bred from a variety of early terriers, with the possible addition of some Whippet blood, the Manchester was originally used as a ratter. Today it is popular as a pet; it has a feisty, energetic nature but lacks the combative edge shown by many other terriers, and usually gets along well with other dogs. Originally a toy version was included in the same standard; now it is shown as a separate dog, although it is still known as the Toy Manchester in the United States.

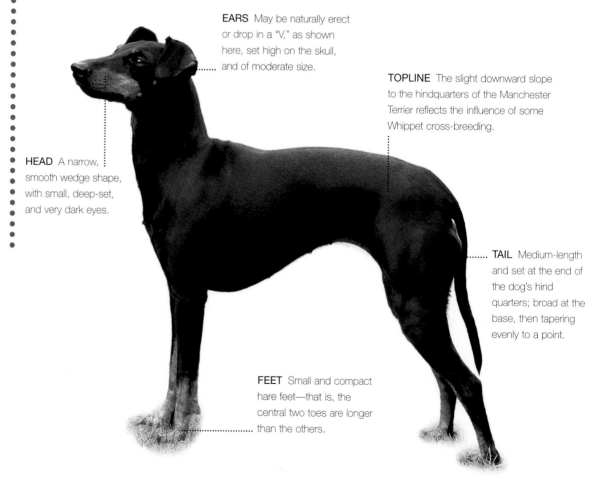

EARS May be naturally erect or drop in a "V," as shown here, set high on the skull, and of moderate size.

TOPLINE The slight downward slope to the hindquarters of the Manchester Terrier reflects the influence of some Whippet cross-breeding.

HEAD A narrow, smooth wedge shape, with small, deep-set, and very dark eyes.

TAIL Medium-length and set at the end of the dog's hind quarters; broad at the base, then tapering evenly to a point.

FEET Small and compact hare feet—that is, the central two toes are longer than the others.

Norfolk Terrier

Lively, feisty, and insatiably curious, the Norfolk Terrier was one of a number of breeds originating in East Anglia, in eastern England, for rabbiting and ratting. Originally it was classed together with the Norwich Terrier (the Norwich, also from eastern England, has prick ears) but was recognized as a separate breed in 1964. This little dog has its fair share of terrier self-confidence; if kept as a pet, its particular enthusiasm for digging may need to be curbed.

NORFOLK TERRIER FACTS

SIZE Dog, height at shoulder, 10–12 in (25–30 cm); bitch, height at shoulder, 9–11 in (23–28 cm).

APPEARANCE A sturdy, lively little dog, solidly balanced on its four short legs.

COAT Thick double coat in shades of red, wheat, tan, and grizzle, sometimes with white markings. The coat is tradtionally "pulled" rather than trimmed, an operation that needs to be carried out by a professional groomer.

BREED HEALTH Generally healthy but can suffer from skin allergies and sometimes back problems.

AN OWNER NEEDS... Time for outdoor exercise, and an inclusive attitude. This little dog likes to be closely involved in whatever is going on and has a cheerful, energetic, and equable approach to life.

TAIL Carried upright and naturally of medium length, although originally docked in working dogs.

BODY Strong and broad-chested, giving the dog a solid but not heavy appearance.

EARS "V" shaped drop ears, thin, and covered with short, smooth fur, falling forward against the cheeks.

EYES Small, dark, and oval with an appealing, lively alert expression.

Toy Dogs

Most toy dogs are, by definition, tiny, but many don't recognize their size, delivering powerful personalities in very small packages. Within this group, however, there is quite a range of character traits, from the extremely feisty to the relatively placid, as well as a variety of appearances, from furry and fluffy—the Papillon or the Shih Tzu—to the small dog, such as the Italian Greyhound, that is simply a miniaturized version of its bigger original.

Yorkshire Terrier

YORKSHIRE TERRIER FACTS

SIZE Dog or bitch, height at shoulder, 7–9 in (18–23 cm).

APPEARANCE The lavish, flowing coat covers a tiny but well-proportioned and solid dog.

COAT Although it is often seen clipped short, the Yorkie's coat is its most distinguishing feature. Long and silky all over the body and head, it comes in one colorway only—a dark steel blue all over the body, from the back of the head to the base of the tail, with a rich tan head, chest, and feet.

BREED HEALTH Yorkshire Terriers have some susceptibility to thyroid and liver disease and hip-joint problems. Like many toy dogs, they can also suffer from tooth decay, and need regular veterinary dental checks.

AN OWNER NEEDS... An awareness that the Yorkshire Terrier is not just a lap dog, and needs play sessions and one-to-one attention, plus a willingness either to spend a long time grooming their dog, or an acceptance of their Yorkie with a shorter, "utility cut."

Opinion is divided as to whether this popular toy dog is first and foremost a terrier or a lap dog. A comparatively recent breed, it was developed over the last century by cross-breeding small terriers, which worked as ratters in the mines of Yorkshire, with Skye Terriers. It is possible that other breeds, including the Dandie Dinmont and the Maltese, also played a part in its creation. The result is a tiny dog, but one that still has plenty of fire in its character.

Commonly known as the Yorkie, this little dog certainly doesn't think of itself as a toy, nor, apparently, does it have any awareness of its size. Most Yorkshire Terriers have all the attitude of their larger terrier brethren and it can be amusing to watch them as they take on the world around them with energy, vigor, and enthusiasm. It can also become occasionally unnerving if your tiny Yorkshire Terrier attempts to take on a dog at least ten times times its size.

From its introduction as a breed—the Yorkshire Terrier was recognized by the Kennel Club of Great Britain in 1886 and had made its way to America by the turn of the last century—the Yorkie won a good deal of popularity as a pet, and it regularly features in the top ten most popular breeds in the Kennel Club's annual survey, usually placing only just behind the Labrador.

The Yorkie's energetic approach to life means that it can make a suitable family dog, as well as a one-person pet, provided that it is kept clear of very small children who may manhandle it—not a good idea for either party, as the dog is too small for rough handling and the child may be rewarded with a nip. This terrier is perfectly able for vigorous exercise, and, for obvious reasons, does not need an immense area to play in, so it is equally appropriate for both city and country dwellers.

Grooming is the main concern for Yorkie owners, as its long and silky coat does need regular and rigorous combing to keep it free of knots and tangles. It also needs to be tied up on top of the dog's head to enable it to see out. If the grooming proves too demanding, one solution is to clip the dog to a manageable length all over—known to groomers as the "utility cut."

TOPKNOT The silky coat forms a thick fringe over the eyes, so most owners opt to tie the dog's hair up in a band or bow to enable it to see out.

EARS Small, upright "V-" shaped ears are set close to the top of the head. The hair on the ears is naturally long, but may be trimmed to neaten the appearance for showing.

TOPLINE The well-arched neck leads down to a straight, rather short back.

TAIL Customarily docked in the past, although this practice is now banned in the UK and some European countries. Carried in a short curve above the topline of the back.

HEAD The skull is flat between the ears, and descends to a small, shortish muzzle. The nose is black.

LEGS Fine but well-boned and not weak; viewed straight on, both front and rear legs are straight. Feet are rounded in shape.

Cavalier King Charles Spaniel

CAVALIER KING CHARLES SPANIEL FACTS

SIZE Dog or bitch, height at shoulder, 12–13 in (30.5–33 cm).

APPEARANCE A neat and attractive silhouette, rather short in the face, with long, decorative, fringed ears and a soft, rather melting expression.

COAT A silky, medium-length coat that may be wavy, but which should not curl. The chest, legs, tail, and ears are all heavily fringed. There are four color combinations, each with its own name—Black and Tan is black with tan markings; Ruby is solid, rich chestnut red; Blenheim is white with chestnut markings, and Tricolor is black on a white ground with tan marks over the eyes, on the cheeks, chest, legs, and underneath the tail.

BREED HEALTH Prone to a number of congenital conditions, including weak knees and heart murmurs. There is a high incidence of mitral valve disease, a serious inherited heart problem. If obtaining a puppy, check with the breeder that the breeding stock is clear.

AN OWNER NEEDS... To give this dog the affection and attention it craves, along with regular exercise and grooming.

Not to be confused with the slightly smaller King Charles Spaniel (known as the English Toy Spaniel in the United States), the Cavalier King Charles comes from a long tradition of miniature spaniels that were popular pets from the 16th century onward—the name is taken from Charles II, at whose court these dogs were well known. The true origins of the Cavalier are believed to lie much further afield, in Japan, but they were well known in Europe by the 1500s.

While larger spaniels were being used as retrievers, their smaller, shorter-faced cousins, such as the Cavalier, were being bred solely as toy dogs. However, the current Cavalier is one of the largest of today's toy breeds.

This dog has long been in demand as a family pet, and it's not hard to see why. Gentle, spirited, and graceful, the Cavalier fits into most surroundings. It will be equally happy with a family or a single owner, and will easily adapt to living in the town or the country, in a house or an apartment. Cavaliers have a cheerful, easygoing approach to life and enjoy human company. They love children and are tolerant of their attentions, are friendly with other dogs and get along with cats and other household pets. Their exercise needs are moderate (although Cavaliers will enthusiastically join you on a long walk if you want one), and although they need regular grooming, the coat is not particularly demanding to keep in good condition. These dogs need plenty of attention and company—human or canine—to thrive, and should not be left alone for long periods. Amenable and easy to train, this breed is also an appropriate choice for a relatively inexperienced owner.

The Cavalier's great popularity means it has a higher-than-average number of inherited health conditions. Conscientious breeders are careful about their stock and are continually checking to ensure that any health problems are not bred on in their puppies, so if you are thinking of acquiring a Cavalier, check with the breeder about the health record of his or her stock.

EARS This puppy has not yet fully developed the heavily fringed and very deep drop ear that is characteristic of the breed, but its ears already fall to chin level.

HEAD The Cavalier's skull is less domed than that of the King Charles Spaniel. Its large, round, dark eyes give the dog a sweet expression.

NECK Long enough to enable the dog to carry its head proudly, and slightly arched.

BODY A balanced ribcage in proportion with the build and size of the dog. The topline is straight from the base of the neck to the tail.

TAIL In adults, the tail develops heavy pluming. It is carried level with or slightly above the dog's back.

FEET The paws are round and compact with deep, thick pads. The long fur that grows between the pads on the underside of the paw is sometimes trimmed to neaten the appearance.

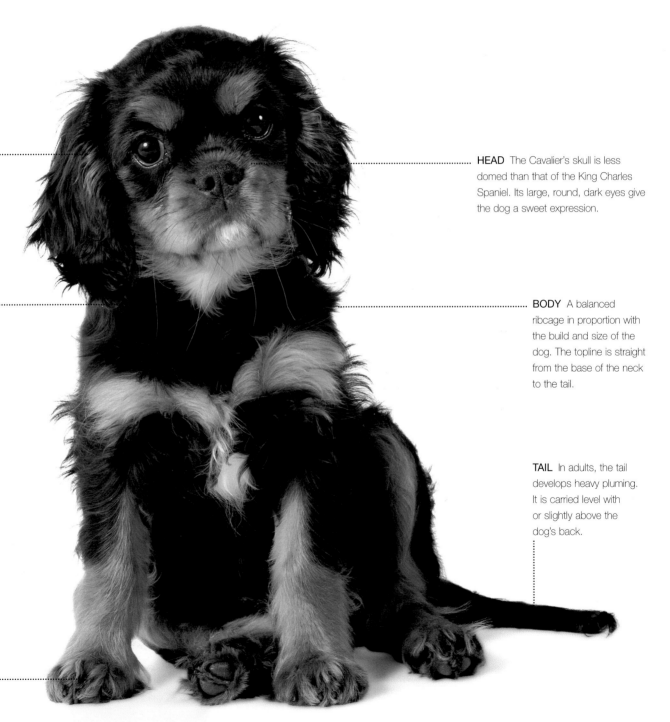

ESSENTIALS EXERCISE 🐾 🐾 GROOMING 🐾 🐾 EASY TO TRAIN 🐾 EXPENSIVE TO KEEP 🐾

Chihuahua

CHIHUAHUA FACTS

SIZE Dog or bitch, height at shoulder, 6–9 in (15–23 cm).

APPEARANCE Fine-boned, though not weak, with a neat, compact outline, a large head with big, erect ears, and a lively, alert expression.

COAT The Chihuahua exists in both short- and longhaired versions; both sometimes have a double coat, sometimes not. The shorthairs have a fine, sleek coat, while the longhairs have thick fur everywhere except on the face and the lower legs. Chihuahuas come in every possible color, and may be solid-, bi-, or tricolored.

BREED HEALTH The size of the Chihuahua means that it is automatically more delicate than some other breeds, and cannot tolerate rough handling. Otherwise, this dog has susceptibilities to progressive retinal atrophy (an eye disease), sometimes weak knees, and there are occasional instances of hydrocephalus, because one of the oddities of the Chihuahua is that the front plates of its skull, open at birth, never quite close up.

AN OWNER NEEDS... To understand that, tiny though it is, this dog still needs training. A sense of humor is also needed, to deal with the Chihuahua's undeniable self-importance.

The Chihuahua is the world's tiniest dog—although sometimes it seems that the only living thing not to recognize this fact is the dog itself. Lively, energetic and terrier-like in its tenacity, this minute creature possesses one of the more powerful canine personalities. The Chihuahua may be small, but those around it will always know it is there. Today, it is one of the most popular of the toy breeds, although its origins are still much debated.

Theories about its background range from claims that it was once the sacred breed of the Aztecs (or, in a variant of the story, the Pharaohs), to tales about its ancient European heritage in Malta. There aren't many definite facts to back up any of these claims, but the Chihuahua is named after the state in Mexico from where the first examples were exported to the United States early in the 20th century. While the Chihuahua became immediately popular in the United States, the dog only caught on as a breed in Europe and the UK in the late 1960s; it now, however, has equal appreciation on both sides of the Atlantic.

Wherever it came from originally, today the Chihuahua is firmly entrenched both as a pet and a show dog. Despite its delicate looks, it does not need any very special care, although it should not be subjected to the company of children too young to understand the careful handling such a small animal needs. Its grooming requirements are minimal, and it is inexpensive to feed.

Personality-wise, the Chihuahua will offer its owners endless entertainment as they watch it organize things around it to its best advantage. Affectionate with its immediate carers, it can also be jealous of its owner's attention, and will do whatever it deems necessary to ensure that it gets the respect and admiration that it feels it deserves. It is worth taking some time to train a Chihuahua properly as, despite its size, its wilful streak means that it can become a nuisance unless it understands at least the basics of polite behavior. It is also essential to socialize it properly with other dogs—otherwise you run the risk of the combative element in its personality appearing at the most inconvenient moments.

EARS Triangular and very large in proportion to the size of the dog. Carried upright and facing forward when alert.

NOSE Matches the coat color in the paler shades, as here, or black with the darker-colored coats.

HEAD A high, rounded skull is a particular characteristic of this breed. Because the plates of the skull never entirely fuse, the Chihuahua is particularly vulnerable to head injuries.

TAIL Long, tapering only a little, and carried in a confident curve. The longhaired variety has a heavily plumed tail.

HINDQUARTERS Well-developed and muscular, adding to the compact yet refined overall appearance.

FEET Small, delicate paws with well-divided and arched toes.

ESSENTIALS   EXERCISE 🐾   GROOMING 🐾   EASY TO TRAIN 🐾 🐾   EXPENSIVE TO KEEP 🐾

Papillon

PAPILLON FACTS

SIZE Dog or bitch, height at shoulder, 8–11 in (20–23 cm).

APPEARANCE Delicate and elegant, with extremely characteristic ears and neat, fine-boned legs.

COAT A single, silky coat, longer on the body and with a profuse "bib" on the chest; short and fine on the head and the lower legs. Always white with patches of a second color.

BREED HEALTH Papillons are sturdy little dogs, but may suffer from slipping knee caps, epilepsy, and some eye and teeth problems.

AN OWNER NEEDS... To be prepared to keep its Papillon company, and deal with its very moderate grooming and exercise needs. Patience is needed to wait for a puppy—demand tends to outstrip supply.

Despite its name—"*papillon*" means "butterfly" in French, in reference to the dog's wing-like ears—this breed actually has Spanish origins, and is believed to have been kept as a lap dog at the Spanish court. It probably originated from a number of toy spaniel breeds, now extinct. It was first shown in Britain in the 1920s, and in the United States a decade later. This popular pet is friendly, companionable, and less highly strung than many other toy dogs.

EYES Dark and round, set in dark rims, of medium size and with a lively, vigilant expression.

EARS The most notable characteristic of this decorative little breed: large with pointed tips, and held forward and very erect, like the wings of a butterfly.

FACE Fine and neat, with a tapered muzzle. The nose is always black. The markings shown here—a white stripe and muzzle dividing an otherwise black face—is quite common.

TOPLINE Very straight, even, and level.

TAIL Well-plumed and carried curled over the back and resting against one side of the body.

LEGS Slender, with straight forelegs and long feet of the hare type—the central two toes longer than the rest.

ESSENTIALS **EXERCISE** 🐾 **GROOMING** 🐾 🐾 **EASY TO TRAIN** 🐾 **EXPENSIVE TO KEEP** 🐾 🐾

Italian Greyhound

Like many other toy breeds, the Italian Greyhound appears, at first glance, simply to be a smaller and more delicate variation on the full-size model. Its character, gentle, and sometimes rather timid, matches its appearance and it will do best with an owner who can give it a peaceful home and calm handling. These dogs enjoy exercise and are very fast sprinters, but are sensitive to the cold, and need to wear coats when outside in chilly weather.

ITALIAN GREYHOUND FACTS

SIZE Dog or bitch, height at shoulder, 13–15 in (33–38 cm).

APPEARANCE A very elegant and graceful dog, with an extremely slender greyhound outline. The overall impression should be one of refinement without weakness.

COAT Short and fine, neat-fitting and very glossy. In a range of colors and color mixes, including black, tan, red, and creamy white. Brindle markings and black with tan markings are not allowed under the breed standard.

BREED HEALTH Subject to a range of problems, including overactive thyroid, eye weaknesses, and weak knee joints. These little dogs can, however, be very long-lived.

AN OWNER NEEDS... A gentle approach to training and a willingness to indulge its sensitive personality.

EARS Thin and medium in size, with a neat fold. They raise slightly when the dog is excited, but are never fully upright.

EYES Round, large, and dark, giving a sweet expression.

TAIL Long and thin, tapering to a small crook at the end, and carried low, raising slightly when the dog is running.

HEAD Narrow all through the skull, tapering to a fine, elegant muzzle.

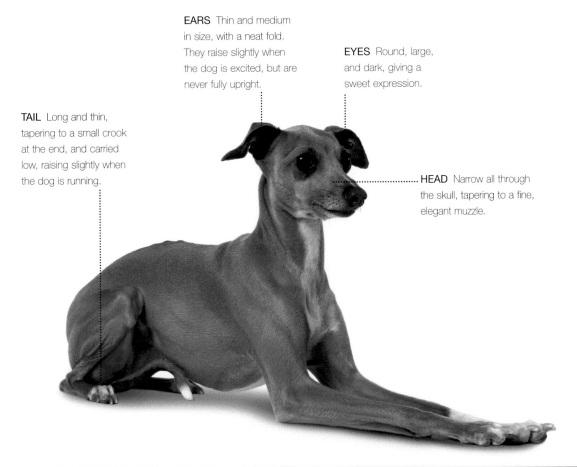

ESSENTIALS   EXERCISE 🐾 🐾   GROOMING 🐾   EASY TO TRAIN 🐾 🐾   EXPENSIVE TO KEEP 🐾 🐾

Miniature Pinscher

MINIATURE PINSCHER FACTS

SIZE Dog or bitch, height at shoulder, 10–12½ in (25–32 cm).

APPEARANCE Tiny but sturdy and in proportion, echoing the attributes of its much larger pinscher cousins. The Miniature Pinscher gives the impression of being a working dog first and a toy dog second.

COAT Short, sleek, and tight-fitting, in a combination of colors: solid tan, tan, or chocolate with rust markings, and black with tan markings—in a very similar arrangement to those of the much larger Doberman.

BREED HEALTH Generally healthy but with some issues, including slipping knee joints, epilepsy, and some heart and eye problems.

AN OWNER NEEDS... Plenty of energy to keep up with this lively and affectionate little dog.

This sturdy toy dog was originally developed in Germany as a small ratting terrier. Originally much larger, it was miniaturized, probably by introducing some Greyhound and possibly also some Dachshund blood. Today known by aficionados as the "min pin," it is an energetic pet in a compact package, always ready for a game or a run. Spirited and lively, it likes to be kept busy, but has an independent personality and can prove challenging to train.

HEAD Narrow and tapering to a sharp muzzle, finished with a black nose, except in the chocolate coloring, in which the nose is dark brown. ....

EARS Large, triangular, and set high on the head. They are carried upright and forward-facing and are very mobile.

TAIL Of medium length .... and carried high and upright. Previously docked in working dogs, although this practice is becoming less common.

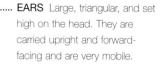

LEGS Strong and well-muscled in relation to the size of the dog, these are lifted when the Miniature Pinscher is moving, creating a high-stepping gait like that of a trotting horse.

ESSENTIALS EXERCISE 🐾🐾 GROOMING 🐾🐾 EASY TO TRAIN 🐾🐾🐾🐾 EXPENSIVE TO KEEP 🐾

Pug

Unlike many of the toy breeds, the Pug seems to have originally been bred purely as a companion dog. It was especially popular at the Dutch court in the 17th century and thereafter became fashionable for a time all over Europe. Keen to please, Pugs love to be with people and are easily trained. Their easygoing, cheerful personalities, and limited exercise needs mean that they are well-suited to fit into most kinds of living arrangements.

PUG FACTS

SIZE Dog or bitch, height at shoulder, 10–14 in (25–35.5 cm).

APPEARANCE A solid, rather thickset body is finished by a tightly curling tail at one end and a short-nosed, characterful head at the other.

COAT Short, shiny, and tight-fitting everywhere except on the head and brow, where it falls into a series of wrinkles. Coat colors are solid black, silver, or fawn; the latter two have darker shading around the muzzle and ears.

BREED HEALTH Pugs are prone to problems with their breathing and their eyes. They are also susceptible to heat stroke and great care needs to be taken to ensure they are not over-exerted in hot weather.

AN OWNER NEEDS... The time to give this loving breed plenty of attention. Plus a tolerance of snoring—most Pugs are inveterate snorers.

TAIL This is one of the characteristic features of the Pug, and is arranged to one side of the dog's back in a tight, furry curl.

EARS "V"-shaped, thin, soft and velvety in texture, falling to the side of the head in a neat fold.

HEAD Square and large, heavily wrinkled, and finishing in a very short, blunt muzzle with a black nose.

LEGS Very strong and well-boned, giving the Pug a solid, foursquare stance.

ESSENTIALS   EXERCISE 🐾 🐾   GROOMING 🐾   EASY TO TRAIN 🐾 🐾   EXPENSIVE TO KEEP 🐾

Toy Poodle

TOY POODLE FACTS

SIZE Dog or bitch at shoulder, no more than 10 in (25 cm).

APPEARANCE Neat, balanced proportions, elegant without being fragile or appearing over-refined.

COAT Curly, dense, woolly coat in a wide range of solid colors, including silver, blue-gray, black, brown, apricot (a blondish beige), and cream.

BREED HEALTH The miniaturization of this breed has taken its toll, and the Toy has more of a genetic predisposition to a variety of problems than the larger Poodle types. These include epilepsy, eye problems, heart disease, and the hormonal imbalance known as Addison's disease. For all these reasons, the breeding stock should be carefully checked if you are acquiring a puppy.

AN OWNER NEEDS... To be prepared to give this appealing little dog the personal attention it craves and needs. In exchange, the Toy Poodle will willingly play the part of the ultimate tiny companion dog.

The Poodle is unusual in that it has both Miniature and Toy versions—and the Toy is very small: no taller than 10 in (25 cm) in the breed standard, but often much tinier. In questions other than that of size, the Toy Poodle is very like its larger siblings, spirited, intelligent, and active, with plenty of character. It makes an excellent companion dog, but care must be taken when acquiring one as this tiny dog is prone to far more health problems than the larger Poodle types.

Despite the Standard being bred down to the Miniature, and the Miniature in its turn being bred down to the Toy, the true Poodle personality has managed to remain largely intact. Today, it is one of the most popular of the toy breeds.

The full show clip is a mirror image of that for the larger Poodle types, and costs a good deal to maintain: every six weeks, the dog needs to be professionally and elaborately clipped. This clip has its origins in a practical cut for a dog that was used for retrieving in water, but in an exaggerated form: the bracelets of fur around ankles and knees were intended to keep the dog's joints warm, as was the deep ruff extending from the head down over the chest, while the underside of the body, the upper legs, and the feet were clipped short to give the dog freedom of movement when swimming. If the Poodle is not to be shown, an all-over utility clip—leaving the dog with a short haircut that is of a uniformly even length—every few months is all that is necessary to keep it in good trim. This breed does not shed, so needs some form of regular clip to keep its coat tidy and well maintained. Poodles are often alleged by their large number of fans to be hypo-allergenic—that is, not to spark off allergies in those who are usually allergic to dog hair—but although the hard, woolly coat does seem to give allergy sufferers fewer problems than most dog fur, this isn't universal, and some find that they are as allergic to the poodle as to other breeds.

Toy Poodles can keep up with an active lifestyle and do not have to be coddled; they are keen to learn, can cope with agility courses, master obedience training and, if their owner has the taste for it, they can learn any number of tricks.

HEAD The skull is rounded and leads down, via a short stop, to the long, refined, rather narrow muzzle.

EARS Set level with the eyes, very long and wide, and densely feathered with thick fur.

EYES Widely set, oval, and invariably dark, whatever the coat color of the dog. Very lively and intelligent in expression.

NECK Strong and well-muscled, supporting the upright carriage of the head particularly characteristic of this breed.

LEGS Long and straight, with strongly developed, muscular hindquarters.

FEET Forward facing on both front and hind legs that are small and even in comparison with the overall size of the dog, with arched toes and strong, compact pads.

● ESSENTIALS EXERCISE 🐾 GROOMING 🐾 🐾 🐾 EASY TO TRAIN 🐾 🐾 🐾 EXPENSIVE TO KEEP 🐾 🐾 🐾

Affenpinscher

AFFENPINSCHER FACTS

SIZE Dog or bitch, height at shoulder, 9½–11½ in (24–27 cm).

APPEARANCE A naturally scruffy, clown-like little dog with an amusing, highly animated expression.

COAT Rough and dense, naturally quite short but standing clear of the dog's body. Most commonly seen in black, but there are red, gray, silver, and black-and-tan variations.

BREED HEALTH This dog is difficult to breed from, but once mature has few health problems. There are some instances of hip dysplasia and cataracts.

AN OWNER NEEDS... Enthusiasm for training this independent breed, and for keeping things varied so that the dog does not become bored. This is not a great breed around small children, as it can be nippy.

Literally "monkey-terrier," this odd, short-nosed little dog is an old breed first developed in Germany as a ratter. Although its size puts it into the toy group, it has a terrier-like character—extremely self-possessed and inquisitive, it will visibly assess any situation in which it finds itself and work out how to turn it to its best advantage. It can fit into most surroundings and with most owners, although it may need to be dissuaded from its natural enthusiasm for barking.

HEAD Round, dark eyes and a rather flat face combine with lavish facial hair to give this dog a comical look.

BACK Short, straight, and solid. The Affenpinscher is altogether solidly built for its small size.

TAIL Set high, of fairly even thickness down its length, and carried over its back in a curve.

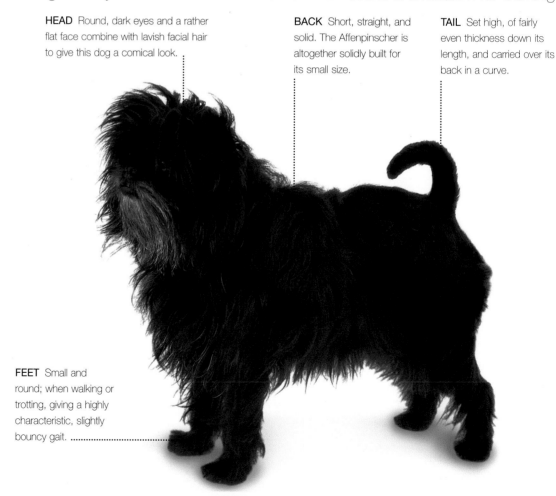

FEET Small and round; when walking or trotting, giving a highly characteristic, slightly bouncy gait.

ESSENTIALS EXERCISE 🐾 🐾 GROOMING 🐾 🐾 EASY TO TRAIN 🐾 🐾 EXPENSIVE TO KEEP 🐾 🐾

Chinese Crested

This extraordinary looking dog became almost extinct in the 1960s, but has been revived as an unusual companion dog by careful breeding. Breed legend asserts that it came from China by way of South America, but this is far from certain. There are two types—the Crested, which is bare-skinned apart from tufts of hair on its ears, head, tail, and feet, and the Powder Puff, which has a full, flowing coat. Both types may be born into the same litter.

CHINESE CRESTED FACTS

SIZE Dog or bitch, height at shoulder, 10–13 in (25–33 cm).

APPEARANCE The Crested has bare skin, often marked with darker, pigmented patches, except for tufts on the head, tail, and feet; the Powder Puff is covered all over with a flowing coat.

COAT The hair on either type is very long and silky, and the Powder Puff has a double coat. The breed standard allows any color or combination of colors.

BREED HEALTH Few inherited health problems, but the crested is highly sensitive to temperature and must be protected from the sun in the summer and the cold in the winter.

AN OWNER NEEDS... To allow for a dog that wants to be with them and only them. Chinese Cresteds are supremely devoted to their owners.

EARS Carried upright and extremely heavily fringed with long, silky hair.

EYES Wide-set, dark, and almond shaped, with an intense, alert expression.

TOPLINE Long and straight, but with a slight downward curve toward the tail.

SKIN The bare skin of the Chinese Crested feels very warm to the touch. These dogs like to be close to their owners, and make excellent lap warmers. The hairless variety should always wear a coat outdoors in even mildly cold weather, and protective sunscreen on warmer days.

FEET This breed has hare feet, with the two central toes longer than the rest.

ESSENTIALS   EXERCISE   GROOMING   EASY TO TRAIN   EXPENSIVE TO KEEP

Pekingese

PEKINGESE FACTS

SIZE Dog or bitch, height at shoulder, 6–9 in (15–23 cm).

APPEARANCE Beneath all the flowing hair is a solid and somewhat stocky dog with a very short face and a rather serious bearing.

COAT An extremely long double coat with a straight top layer, coarse rather than soft in texture, and a dense, thick undercoat. All colors are available apart from liver, and the dog usually has a dark or black "mask," regardless of the color of its coat.

BREED HEALTH This dog can be subject to heart and breathing conditions, dislocated and slipped kneecaps and disks, and various eye conditions including trichaiasis (ingrowing eyelashes). If you are buying a puppy, it is crucial to check the health of the breeding stock with the breeder.

AN OWNER NEEDS... The patience to train this independent little dog, and the strength of mind to deal with its occasional obstinacy. Pekingese don't need much exercise, but they do need some, and they are not always enthusiastic walkers, so an owner may need to encourage them. Time will need to be spent on daily grooming to keep the distinctive coat in good condition.

While the distant origins of these dogs are not known, by the late 18th century they were being kept at the Chinese court as companions to the Imperial family. No-one below royal status was allowed to keep a Pekingese; it was believed that they were the physical manifestations of the mythical Fu dogs, the lion-like guardians of China. The tiniest examples were carried in the trailing sleeves of court robes, and the breed was not known outside China.

All this changed when the Imperial Palace in Beijing was raided by the British army in the 1860s. Although orders were issued to kill the court dogs to prevent them falling into enemy hands, five Pekingese were found and were brought back to England as curiosities, where one was presented to Queen Victoria. This little group formed the core breed stock of the Pekingese in the West, and it was registered with the British Kennel Club in 1893, and in America in 1909.

Today, the Peke, as it is known, is a popular pet and a regular attendee in the show ring. It has a distinctive, rather dignified personality, with an independent streak. It can be stubborn in training (and owners report that if it is crossed it can sulk in a rather human way), but it is also spirited and game to join in with whatever activity is on offer. It has the self-assurance of many of the other toy breeds, and can be combative with other dogs on first meeting, but can usually get along with other household pets if carefully introduced.

Unlike many other breeds, Pekingese can sometimes be notably averse to exercise and may also be rather fussy about their food. Even if the Peke is unwilling to move around much, its owners should accustom it to at least a short daily walk, and find a balanced diet that suits its sometimes rather picky tastes to ensure that this often long-lived breed stays fit and healthy. The full coat can be punishing in hot weather, and dogs must be kept cool with plenty of shade or, if not show dogs, clipped to help them tolerate high temperatures. This is also a breed that can suffer a number of inherited health problems, so time should be taken when acquiring a Peke to check that it comes from sound breeding stock.

EYES Dark in all coat colors, large and rather round. They should be prominent, but not protuberant or bulging. Eye rims are black, as is the surrounding skin.

HEAD A broad, flat, heavy skull means that the face is wider than it is deep when seen head-on. The very flat muzzle is covered in short, black fur.

JAW Like some other flat-faced breeds, the Peke's jaw is undershot. The mouth should close neatly; a common fault is that teeth or tongue show when the mouth is shut, and this is penalized in a showdog.

COAT This Pekingese puppy is just starting to develop the extremely profuse coat that is such a strong characteristic of the breed. Its shorter fur, however, does show the subtle color shading typical of the Peke.

LEGS The front legs are somewhat bowed and very strongly made, and the front paws turn outward a little. The rear legs are much lighter in bone, and the feet face forward.

ESSENTIALS EXERCISE 🐾 GROOMING 🐾🐾🐾 EASY TO TRAIN 🐾🐾🐾 EXPENSIVE TO KEEP 🐾🐾

Maltese

MALTESE FACTS

🐾 **SIZE** Dog or bitch, height at shoulder, 8–10 in (20–25 cm).

🐾 **APPEARANCE** Small and solid, with a refined face, and an extremely luxurious coat.

🐾 **COAT** A single coat, but very fine, thick, and long. The only color is pure white, although there may be light lemon markings on the ears.

🐾 **BREED HEALTH** Generally healthy, although skin sensitivities and allergies are common. Care should be taken that the dog does not become overheated in warm weather.

🐾 **AN OWNER NEEDS...** To be prepared for a loving companion that will happily act as their "shadow," the Maltese likes to be close to its owner. Grooming is also time consuming unless you go for a shorter, utility cut.

Cheerful and affectionate, the Maltese seems to have a good understanding of its status as a toy dog, and is happy simply accompanying its owners wherever they go. This is one of the oldest European breeds, and was popular as a lap dog at many royal courts by the 16th century. Today, it is a successful pet and show dog, fitting in easily with a wide variety of lifestyles.

HEAD A slightly rounded skull tapers to a muzzle that is refined but not too pointed or narrow. The nose is black.

EARS Low-set drop ears, covered in heavy feathering and hanging close to the head. This puppy's ears will grow longer as it matures.

EYES Large, round, dark, and soft in expression, rimmed with black and set moderately far apart.

LEGS Fine boned and also heavily feathered with silky fur. The paws are small, round, and neat.

ESSENTIALS   **EXERCISE** 🐾   **GROOMING** 🐾 🐾 🐾 🐾   **EASY TO TRAIN** 🐾 🐾   **EXPENSIVE TO KEEP** 🐾 🐾

Shih Tzu

The Shih Tzu strongly resembles its larger cousin, the Lhasa Apso, which originated in Tibet—and the most likely theory about its origin proposes that it was the result of crossing a Lhasa Apso with a Pekingese. It was a valued dog in Imperial China and was first imported to the West in the 1930s, since when it has achieved success as a pet. Its cheerful, sociable, and lively character makes this little dog deservedly popular.

SHIH TZU FACTS

SIZE Dog or bitch, height at shoulder, 9–11 in (23–28 cm).

APPEARANCE A compact body with a notably upright carriage of the head, covered all over with a long double coat.

COAT A flowing topcoat over a short, dense undercoat, in any solid color or combination of colors. The fringe is usually tied up in a topknot to enable the dog to see out.

BREED HEALTH Generally strong and healthy, Shih Tzus can suffer from hip dysplasia and have some predisposition to eye and kidney infections.

AN OWNER NEEDS... The patience to groom the high-maintenance coat, or to be prepared to clip it short, plus enough time to meet the Shih Tzu's modest exercise needs and to enjoy its perky temperament.

HEAD Broad, with a short muzzle and large, dark, wide-set eyes, giving the dog a sweet, lively expression.

TOPLINE Level for the full length of the short, sturdy body.

TAIL Extremely lavishly plumed, set rather high, and carried in a curve over the dog's back.

NECK Muscular and with a strong upright curve, allowing the Shih Tzu's naturally high, proud head carriage.

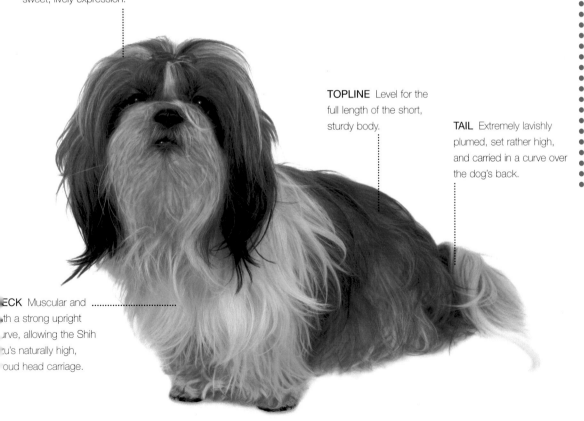

ESSENTIALS   **EXERCISE** 🐾   **GROOMING** 🐾 🐾 🐾   **EASY TO TRAIN** 🐾   **EXPENSIVE TO KEEP** 🐾 🐾

Brussels Griffon

BRUSSELS GRIFFON FACTS

🐾 **SIZE** Dog or bitch, height at shoulder, 8–10 in (20–25 cm).

🐾 **APPEARANCE** A small but solid and substantial dog with a sturdy build, and a characterful face boasting a heavy beard and mustache and a lively, rather quizzical expression.

🐾 **COAT** A single coat that may be either smooth or wiry, but never a mixture of the two. The smooth version is tight-fitting and shiny; the rough is tough and wiry. There are four color variations: russet red with some black on the face, solid black, black with tan markings, and beige, made from a mixture of black and brown hairs, usually with a black mask on the face.

🐾 **BREED HEALTH** The Brussels Griffon is a tough and healthy little dog with few inherited health concerns, although it can suffer from eye and breathing problems. However, it is especially difficult to breed, so it can prove difficult to locate the source for a puppy.

🐾 **AN OWNER NEEDS...** The time to train this independent-minded dog and an awareness of its sometimes rather nervous personality: it can be somewhat shy, and needs consistent, encouraging handling and socializing to turn it into a reliable pet.

The Brussels Griffon is, today, categorized and shown in both smooth and rough-coated varieties in the UK and the United States. Confusingly, however, in Europe the two types are shown as separate breeds, the smooth-coated dog being known as the Petit Brabancon. Apart from their coats, the dogs are identical: small and substantial with extremely expressive little faces and determined, somewhat terrier-like, characters.

The terrier-like aspect is not surprising, because these little dogs were bred as ratters: in the days of horse-drawn carriages they were well known in the stables of Brussels where they were kept specifically for the purpose. There is a wide variety of theories about which breeds went into the making of the modern Griffon, but it seems likely that small terriers were among their recent ancestors, and there may also have been some cross-breeding with Pug dogs.

Because of the difficulties the Brussels Griffon has in breeding, it has never become a very widespread or popular pet. This has spared it from some of the inherited health problems of extremely popular breeds, in which poor specimens are bred along with good ones, and it is a sturdy little dog that can live into its teens. While it is not high-strung, the Griffon does need careful, gentle training and socializing that complements its naturally independent and sometimes reserved nature. It is a breed that is famously hard and slow to house-train, so may call for more patience in its owner in this particular area than most other dogs.

The rough-coated Griffon is hand-pulled rather than clipped when the dog is prepared for showing, and this can be expensive, although pets for whom there are no dog-show plans can simply be hand trimmed or kept tidy and comfortable with regular brushing. The smooth-coated variety needs very little grooming.

While the exercise needs of the Griffon are relatively modest, these little dogs are tirelessly inquisitive and need to be kept occupied. Their almost human expression as they keep an eye on their owners' activities is very endearing.

EARS Small drop ears set quite high on the dog's head. It was traditional to crop them to a point in working dogs, but cropped ears are now rarely seen, and cropping is illegal in many European countries.

TOPLINE Straight and sloping very slightly downward toward the hindquarters.

TAIL Carried upright, the natural tail is of medium length but was docked very short in working dogs. This practice is now gradually dying out.

HEAD A high, slightly domed skull leading to a short muzzle and finished with a large black nose.

CHEST Deep, and moderately broad, matching the breed's sturdy, muscular look.

LEGS Straight and strong, with front-facing compact feet with rounded pads and well-arched toes.

ESSENTIALS   EXERCISE 🐾 🐾   GROOMING 🐾 🐾   EASY TO TRAIN 🐾 🐾 🐾   EXPENSIVE TO KEEP 🐾 🐾

Non-Sporting Dogs

The mixed bag of the Kennel Club groups, this section is a catch-all for all the dog breeds that didn't, for one reason or another, quite fit into any of the other classifications. There are some odd stablemates in this category, ranging from the smart Dalmatian and the majestic but serious-minded Chow Chow, to the cuddly Boston Terrier and the cheerful yet independent Shiba Inu.

Boston Terrier

BOSTON TERRIER FACTS

🐾 **SIZE** Dog or bitch, height at shoulder, 14–17 in (35.5–43 cm).

🐾 **APPEARANCE** A neat, active dog with a compact body, a flat, bulldog-type face, and a short tail, usually tightly curled. .

🐾 **COAT** Fine, short, and sleek, in black, brindle, or black with a reddish cast (known to professional breeders as "seal" coloring), all with white markings.

🐾 **BREED HEALTH** Some susceptibility to cataracts and other eye problems, unstable knees, allergies, and congenital deafness. Boston Terriers are also temperature sensitive and should not be heavily exercised in either very hot or very cold weather.

🐾 **AN OWNER NEEDS...** To be able to meet the Boston Terrier's very moderate exercise needs, and to give this affectionate dog plenty of attention. This sociable dog likes to spend time with its people, and doesn't do well if left alone for long periods.

Cheerful, easygoing, and intelligent, this dapper little dog has the nickname of "the American gentleman" among its large number of admirers, a reflection of its good manners and amiability. Developed in Boston by crossbreeding terriers and Bulldogs, early examples were used as fighting dogs but were quickly bred down in size to become companions and pets. The Boston was first shown in 1870, and registered with the American Kennel Club in 1893.

Although never very large, the modern Boston Terrier varies in size sufficiently to have three different weight ranges registered within the breed standard: lightweight (under 15 pounds/6.8 kg), middleweight (15–20 pounds/6.8–9 kg), and heavyweight (20–25 pounds/9–11 kg). Even the largest of these, however, is still a relatively small dog. This breed's smart appearance is emphasized by the arrangement of markings that is considered ideal by breeders—a white blaze between the eyes reaching up over the forehead, a band around the nose, and a white forechest and paws. It is also set apart by its gait—the Boston moves with a neat, fast trotting motion.

The mixture of bulldog blood into the terrier form has removed many of the less desirable but typical terrier traits. This dog isn't usually hyperactive or quick on the draw like so many of the other terrier breeds and, although the Boston can be an exceptionally lively and energetic puppy, it usually mellows in adulthood into a playful but fundamentally laid-back character. It makes a good playmate for older children, but is too small for unsupervised play with younger ones; it is more likely to come to harm through rough handling than they are.

The Boston Terrier does not need much exercise, although it appreciates regular walks and games. It likes to be involved with its owner, and will be happiest if it is included in everyday activities. Intelligent, and curious, it can fit in with most lifestyles, and is easy to keep—the short coat just needs an occasional comb-through. Although this breed has a number of inherited health problems, most can be avoided by obtaining a dog from a careful breeder.

HEAD Rather square with an abbreviated muzzle, with a slight resemblance to that of the Pug, but without any exaggerated skin wrinkles in brow or muzzle.

EARS Triangular in shape and placed at the corners of the skull. Often sit naturally upright, although historically they have been cropped to points. This practice is illegal in the UK and parts of Europe and is becoming less common elsewhere.

EYES Large, round, and very dark, set wide apart on the face, and soft yet alert in expression.

TAIL The Boston Terrier is unusual in having two natural tail types: carried in a tight curl or screw, or in a short, straight, tapered form.

LEGS The forelegs are widely spaced and straight; the back legs, powerful and well-muscled, giving the Boston Terrier its characteristic smart, confident movement.

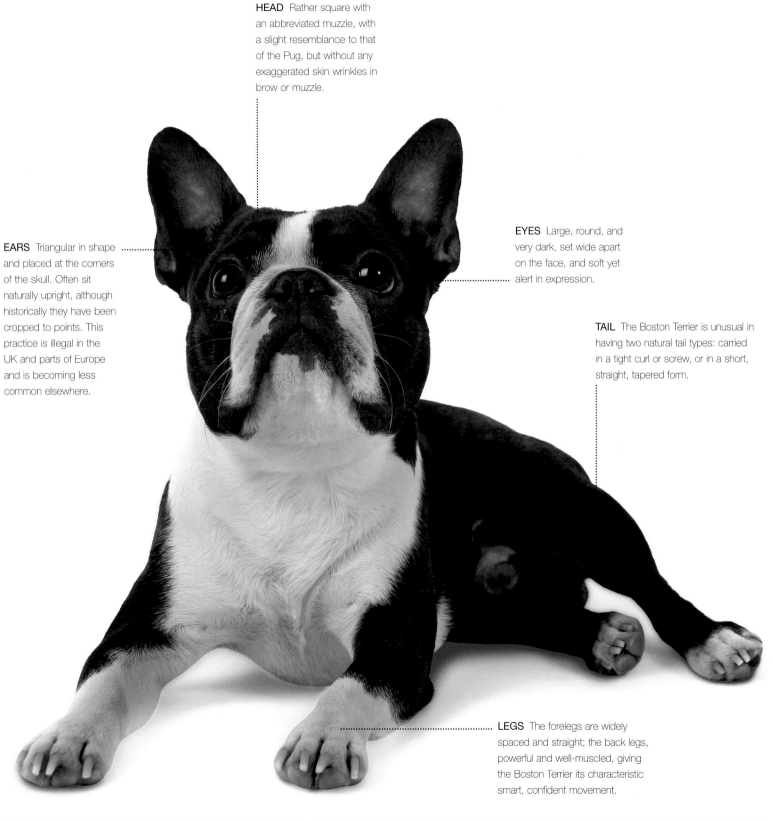

ESSENTIALS   EXERCISE 🐾 🐾   GROOMING 🐾   EASY TO TRAIN 🐾 🐾   EXPENSIVE TO KEEP 🐾 🐾

Dalmatian

DALMATIAN FACTS

SIZE Dog or bitch, height at shoulder, 19–23 in (48–58 cm).

APPEARANCE A balanced, lively, active-looking dog, instantly recognizable by its spotted coat.

COAT Thick, sleek, glossy and fitting tightly to the dog all over without any wrinkles or looseness. Pure white, evenly spotted all over with distinct, round spots, which may be either black or liver-colored, and ideally should be separate and well defined, around an inch across, or slightly smaller.

BREED HEALTH Popularity has been a problem for the Dalmatian. Careless breeding has left some strains with a raft of genetic disorders and susceptibilities, including epilepsy, allergies, hip dysplasia, and hypothyroidism. Deafness also afflicts around one in ten puppies. And, finally, Dalmatians can suffer with a breed-specific allergy-based weeping skin condition known as Dal crud. For all these reasons, it is crucial to buy puppies only from a reputable breeder.

AN OWNER NEEDS... Enough time to train, socialize and exercise this tireless and exuberant breed. Dalmatians can make enchanting pets, but they are also demanding of time and attention.

The Dalmatian's background raises a number of questions, not least of which is how it came by its name. What is known of its history offers no specific connection to Dalmatia, a province in Croatia, Europe—its more likely origins are in the UK, where it was kept as a carriage dog, trotting alongside the horses. Dalmatians are noisy and effective guard dogs and have a particular liking for, and apparently often a special affinity with, horses.

Today, the breed is kept exclusively as a show dog and a pet. Its popularity as the latter soared at the end of the 1950s, as a result of the release of the movie of Dodie Smith's *101 Dalmatians*. Overnight, Dalmatians became massively sought after, and the resulting surge in often irresponsible breeding has left this dog with a range of inherited health problems that responsible breeders are only now beginning to conquer. For this reason, it is very important to acquire a Dalmatian only from a listed, responsible breeder who can vouch for the genetic health of their stock, as well as for its lack of nervousness or aggression. Having obtained a puppy, it is up to the owner to see that it is well looked after and properly socialized.

Dalmatian puppies are born pure white; the spots gradually develop as they mature. The elegance of this dog's appearance can mask its true character: Dalmatians are extremely active, intelligent dogs that can be independent and even wilful thinkers. They may also be slow to train, not because of any absence of brains, but purely because they are easily distracted and will often themselves choose the focus of their attention. The handsome coat sheds heavily and these dogs also need very regular grooming. Finally, Dalmatians are quite noisy dogs and, if at all neglected, may become recreational barkers.

None of this should deter the enthusiast. The Dalmatian is not an inherently difficult dog—just one that keeps its owner up to the mark with regard to its needs. Although this is probably not the best breed for inexperienced owners, a properly trained and regularly and extensively exercised Dalmatian will be a loyal, cheerful, and upbeat companion, and an excellent family dog.

EYES Wide-set and a rounded almond shape, with dark rims. Eyes may be brown or blue, or wall (one eye of each color).

EARS Set high on the head, broad at the base, and narrowing to a pointed tip. Ideally bearing evenly spaced spots, as elsewhere on the dog, but sometimes a solid color, as here.

HEAD A moderately long head, with a flat top to the skull. The muzzle is long and well-modelled, full, without concavity. The nose is large and square, and should be solid black in a black-spotted dog, and solid liver in a liver-spotted one.

NECK Long, strong, well-muscled, and elegant, running smoothly into the dog's shoulders.

CHEST Deep, with broad ribs, adding to the overall powerful appearance of the dog.

FEET Well-sized, rounded, and neat in shape, with strong, flexible, close-set pads and well-arched toes.

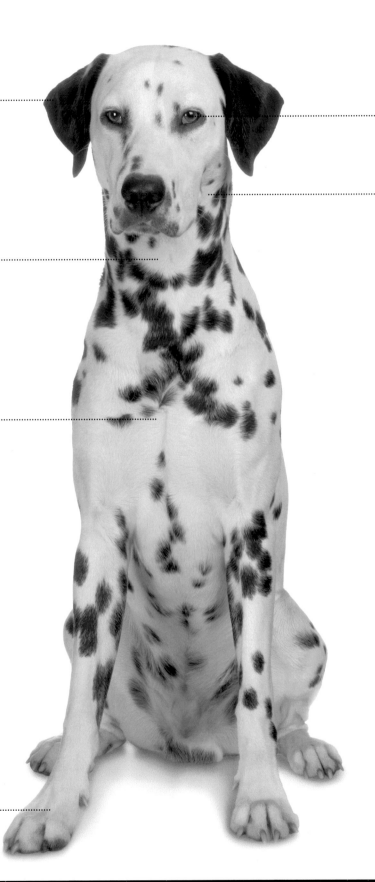

ESSENTIALS EXERCISE 🐾🐾🐾🐾 GROOMING 🐾🐾🐾 EASY TO TRAIN 🐾🐾🐾🐾 EXPENSIVE TO KEEP 🐾🐾🐾

British Bulldog

BULLDOG FACTS

SIZE Dog or bitch, height at shoulder, 12–16 in (30–41 cm).

APPEARANCE A square, low-set dog with an appearance of great power and substance. The face is flat, very wrinkled, and characterful; the demeanor is solemn but gentle.

COAT Short, fine, and shiny, in a range of colors including brindle, red brindle, solid red, white, fawn or brown, or all of these with a black face or muzzle, and piebald (black and white patches).

BREED HEALTH For a dog that has been relentlessly bred to type, the Bulldog has relatively few genetic problems, but those it has are serious: a wide range of breathing conditions, from too-narrow nasal passages to too-narrow a trachea, and severe hip dysplasia. The large head of the Bulldog means that puppies usually have to be delivered by Caesarian section. Even as an adult, this can be a dog that needs a lot of veterinary attention, despite its tough looks.

AN OWNER NEEDS... Sufficient funds and time to cope with the Bulldog's sometimes high medical needs, and to take the trouble to arrive at a good understanding of this endearing but idiosyncratic breed.

Two hundred years ago, the British Bulldog, often chosen to represent the island's national character, looked very different. Bred specifically for bull-baiting and dog fighting, partly from mastiff-type dogs that had been bred for bull-baiting since the 13th century, this exceedingly old breed was specifically developed to be successful in its "sport." It was much longer in the leg, less muscle-bound, more athletic, and altogether more utilitarian in appearance.

When bull-baiting was outlawed in 1835, it looked as though the Bulldog, its working role now redundant, might die out. However, a few enthusiasts kept the breed going, and the first club for Bulldog owners was started in 1875. Within a few decades, the aggressive temperament for which Bulldogs had been known was being gradually bred out, and a more exaggerated outline—big in the head, very heavy-boned and bow-legged—was being bred in. By the 1920s, the Bulldog had the outline that is familiar to us today. The downside of all this concentrated breeding for appearance was that a number of health problems were bred in as well. The list is not hugely long, but it does need attention, and anyone acquiring this sweet-natured breed as a pet needs to be aware of it in order to give their Bulldog the environment and the care it needs.

Today's bulldog is friendly and easygoing. It doesn't have any special problems in training and it is fond of people—it is very affectionate toward those it knows well, and tolerant of strangers, whether human or canine. In terms of care, it needs regular but gentle exercise—bulldogs can't afford to put on weight, as it puts too much strain on the heart, and they can't be exercised much in hot weather as they are extremely temperature sensitive. Most can't swim—their huge heads overbalance them in the water—and some owners train their pets to be water-averse to keep them safe. Bulldogs enjoy having others of their kind for company, and many owners keep a pair. For recreation, most members of this breed are fond of toys, and they love to chew, although owners should remember that toys chosen for a Bulldog have to be tough enough for the job.

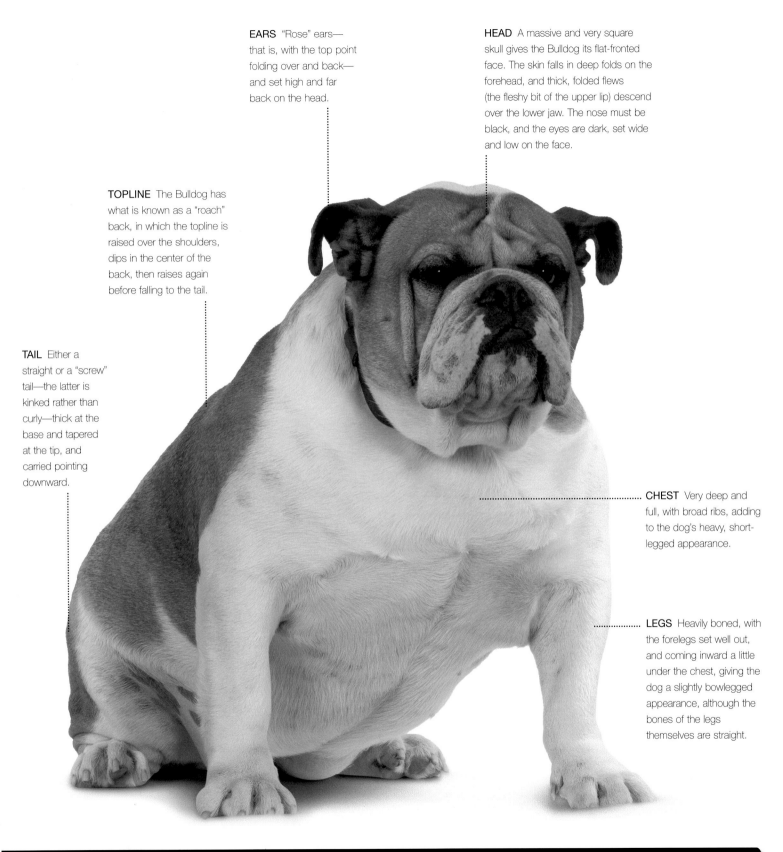

EARS "Rose" ears—that is, with the top point folding over and back—and set high and far back on the head.

HEAD A massive and very square skull gives the Bulldog its flat-fronted face. The skin falls in deep folds on the forehead, and thick, folded flews (the fleshy bit of the upper lip) descend over the lower jaw. The nose must be black, and the eyes are dark, set wide and low on the face.

TOPLINE The Bulldog has what is known as a "roach" back, in which the topline is raised over the shoulders, dips in the center of the back, then raises again before falling to the tail.

TAIL Either a straight or a "screw" tail—the latter is kinked rather than curly—thick at the base and tapered at the tip, and carried pointing downward.

CHEST Very deep and full, with broad ribs, adding to the dog's heavy, short-legged appearance.

LEGS Heavily boned, with the forelegs set well out, and coming inward a little under the chest, giving the dog a slightly bowlegged appearance, although the bones of the legs themselves are straight.

ESSENTIALS EXERCISE 🐾🐾 GROOMING 🐾🐾 EASY TO TRAIN 🐾🐾🐾 EXPENSIVE TO KEEP 🐾🐾🐾🐾

Chinese Shar-Pei

CHINESE SHAR-PEI FACTS

SIZE Dog or bitch, height at shoulder, 18–22 in (46–56 cm).

APPEARANCE Large, strong, and square-bodied, with an unusual coat and face, both covered with deeply wrinkled fold of skin, and an aloof, rather fierce expression.

COAT Very harsh and straight, and, even when healthy, with a matte rather than a shiny finish, in a range of solid colors: black, red, fawn, or cream. Shar-Pei puppies are a mass of wrinkles, but the dogs grow into their skin as they mature, and the wrinkled appearance is reduced.

BREED HEALTH Usually a strong dog, but, as might be expected, the Shar-Pei may suffer from a number of allergic skin conditions. The breed also has a propensity for ingrowing eyelashes and other eye problems. The skin around the face in particular needs regular cleaning to ensure the wrinkles do not trap dirt and cause infection. Finally, Shar-Peis can suffer from a recurrent, breed-specific fever called, appropriately, shar-pei fever.

AN OWNER NEEDS... The time and determination to obedience train this large breed thoroughly and well. Shar-Peis can be stubborn, although once well-trained, they make good and affectionate pets.

A large and stately-looking dog, the Shar-Pei has deeply wrinkled skin, falling in large folds all over its head, chest, and back, ensuring that this is not a dog that will ever be confused with any other breed. Add its face, with more wrinkled padding around the cheeks, mouth, and nose, and you have a breed with unique looks and very ancient origins—lying either in mountainous Tibet or in the northernmost parts of China.

As recently as the 1990s, this eccentric-looking dog was regularly described as "the rarest breed in the world," but in the last decade it has gained popularity, first as a show dog and, more recently, as an unusual but lovable companion and pet.

Originally bred as a fighting dog—in fact, when first imported to the West it was known as the Chinese Fighting Dog—the Shar-Pei was also used as a powerful hunting companion, and as a guardian for livestock. The heavily wrinkled coat had a practical purpose: it was hard for a fighting opponent to get hold of, and if the dog was seized, it still had room enough within its skin to turn on its attacker. The name "Shar-Pei" is believed to be a corruption of a Chinese expression meaning "sand-skin", which is an accurate description of the harsh, matte texture of the Shar-Pei's coat.

This is a dog with an expression that can be hard to read, concealed as it is by a mass of deep wrinkles, but it has plenty of character. The breed standard describes its attitude as "snobbish" and breeders state the dog has an "arrogant" outlook. Despite these negative-sounding descriptions, a properly trained and socialized Shar-Pei becomes utterly dedicated to its family and, with those it knows, can be playful and affectionate. Even a well-trained dog, however, is likely to remain suspicious of and aloof with strangers, and cautious, if not aggressive, around unknown dogs. Given the power of this fighting breed, good training is essential in a Shar-Pei that is to be kept as a pet.

In terms of care, the wrinkled coat needs regular brushing and cleaning. This dog, however, requires only a moderate amount of exercise.

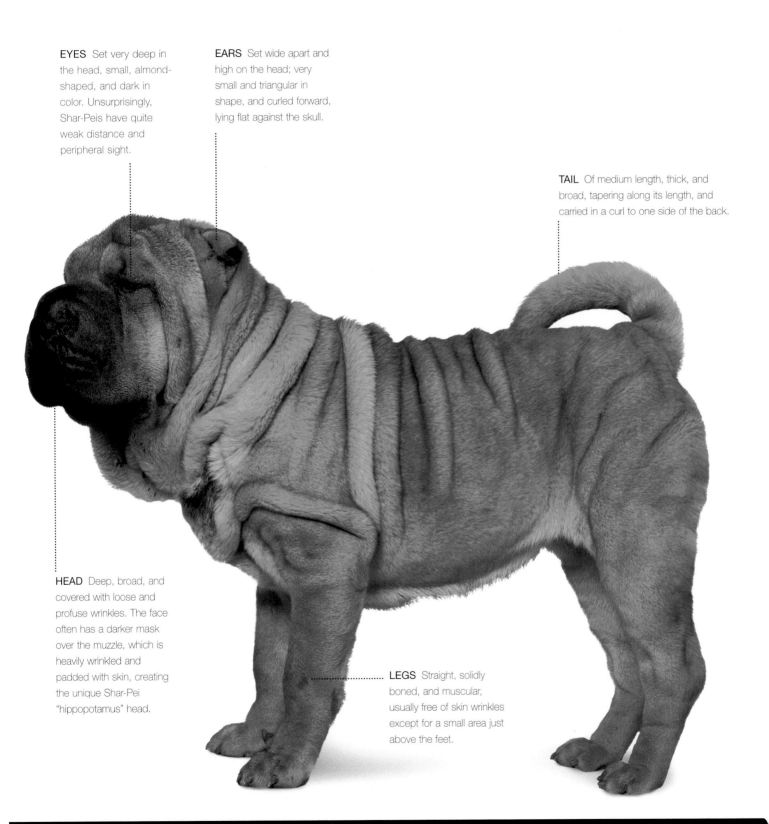

EYES Set very deep in the head, small, almond-shaped, and dark in color. Unsurprisingly, Shar-Peis have quite weak distance and peripheral sight.

EARS Set wide apart and high on the head; very small and triangular in shape, and curled forward, lying flat against the skull.

TAIL Of medium length, thick, and broad, tapering along its length, and carried in a curl to one side of the back.

HEAD Deep, broad, and covered with loose and profuse wrinkles. The face often has a darker mask over the muzzle, which is heavily wrinkled and padded with skin, creating the unique Shar-Pei "hippopotamus" head.

LEGS Straight, solidly boned, and muscular, usually free of skin wrinkles except for a small area just above the feet.

ESSENTIALS EXERCISE 🐾 🐾 GROOMING 🐾 🐾 🐾 EASY TO TRAIN 🐾 🐾 🐾 🐾 EXPENSIVE TO KEEP 🐾 🐾 🐾 🐾

Shiba Inu

SHIBA INU FACTS

🐾 **SIZE** Dog, height at shoulder, 14½–16½ in (37–42 cm); bitch, height at shoulder, 13½–15½ in (35–40 cm).

🐾 **APPEARANCE** A neat, attractive lively dog with a pretty, fox-like face.

🐾 **COAT** A double coat, with a thick, soft underlayer and a straight topcoat that stands out from the dog's body. Colors are red, black and tan or sesame (red wtih black-tipped hairs). The paler contrast pattern on the coat is called *urajiro* in Japan.

🐾 **BREED HEALTH** Generally sound, but with some tendency to have eye problems, slipping knee joints, and epilepsy.

🐾 **AN OWNER NEEDS...** The time and energy to train this energetic and independent-minded breed, and thoroughly socialize it.

One of the most popular pet breeds in Japan, the Shiba Inu was first imported to the West in the 1970s, and is growing in popularity in the United States and the UK, too. This attractive dog was originally bred for hunting and can be somewhat independent-minded but, when trained, makes a lively family dog. It has fastidious habits and can often be seen grooming itself.

TAIL Thickly furred and worn on a single curl over the center of the back.

EARS Open and triangular, set high on the head, well apart, and with a slight forward tilt.

HEAD Broad at the cheeks, with expressive black eyes of triangular shape, tapering slightly to a neat muzzle.

URAJIRO A Japanese word that describes the precise pattern of the contrast hair on the dog's face and front. The fur appears almost shaded between the two colors, creating a subtle effect.

PAWS Neat, rounded feet of the cat type, with high, arched toes.

Chow Chow

Chows have been bred in their native China as hunting dogs for at least 2,000 years; they were also used for their meat and their fur. Bred in the West from the mid-19th century, the Chow is emphatically not for the inexperienced owner—this handsome, aloof dog needs firm, gentle, sustained training and is uninterested in strangers; it can also be aggressive with other dogs.

CHOW CHOW FACTS

SIZE Dog, height at shoulder, 19–22 in (48–56 cm); bitch, height at shoulder, 18–20 in (46–51 cm).

APPEARANCE A large, solid, sturdy foursquare dog with a signature curled tail, extremely muscular in build.

COAT Double coated, and comes in two different types: rough and smooth. Both have the same thick undercoat, but the rough has outer fur with a harsher, rougher texture. The Chow comes in solid colors only: black, red, blue-gray, fawn, and cream.

BREED HEALTH The Chow has a bad record for hip and elbow dysplasia, slipping knee caps, and eye disorders. For this reason, puppies should only be obtained through a carefully chosen breeder.

AN OWNER NEEDS... To be at least as strong minded as this very determined dog.

HEAD Large and carried very high, with a characteristic frowning expression, and very deep-set eyes. The tongue, unusually, is blue-black.

EARS Set widely apart, at the corners of the dog's head; small, triangular, and carried upright at a slight forward slant.

TAIL Heavily furred, set high, and carried in a curve along the line of the back.

LEGS Strong and well-boned. The Chow's back legs are very straight, which gives the dog a rather stiff, measured gait.

ESSENTIALS   EXERCISE 🐾 🐾   GROOMING 🐾 🐾 🐾 🐾 🐾   EASY TO TRAIN 🐾 🐾 🐾 🐾 🐾   EXPENSIVE TO KEEP 🐾 🐾 🐾

French Bulldog

FRENCH BULLDOG FACTS

SIZE Dog or bitch, height at shoulder, 12 in (30 cm) or less.

APPEARANCE A small, short-faced and short-legged dog of unmistakeable bulldog type, with highly distinctive large, upright ears.

COAT A soft, loose, short coat, falling in wrinkles around the face and neck. The texture is fine and shiny, and the colors are solid brindle, fawn, or white, or brindle and white mixed.

BREED HEALTH Generally among the healthiest of the short-faced "bull" breeds, French Bulldogs still sometimes suffer from eye problems (including inturned eyelids and cataracts) and slipping knee joints.

AN OWNER NEEDS... To meet very few specific requirements in comparison with those called for by many other breeds. French Bulldogs are very affectionate, moderately easy to train, and don't need very high levels of exercise (although they still need regular walks). This breed needs company, and won't do well left alone for long periods.

The French Bulldog has a number of theories to offer about its ancestry, but the most convincing is that a number of the smaller bulldogs, kept as pets rather than as fighting dogs, were brought with their owners from England to France when the latter fetched over a number of textile workers in the mid-19th century. The undersized bulldogs bred with French stock, and gradually became the bat-eared, flat-faced French Bulldog that is familiar today.

Other theories tell more or less the same story, but state that the original bulldogs were bred with Spanish stock (or even that purely French and Spanish dogs made the breed). Whichever is true, by the beginning of the 20th century, the French Bulldog had become an extremely fashionable pet on both sides of the Channel, favored by characters as diverse as Edward VII of England and the romantic French novelist, Colette. From about 1910, the breed was attracting attention at shows in the United States. The most immediately recognizable characteristic of the "Frenchie," the large, upright, and endearing bat ears (sometimes known to enthusiasts by the prettier but somehow less expressive name of "tulip" ears), took some time to breed in.

Bred purely to be a companion dog, the French Bulldog has never been used for fighting, like many of the other old, mastiff-originating breeds, and has always been both popular and successful as a pet.

The French Bulldog is one of the healthiest of the bulldog breeds. However, the flat face still means that it is susceptible to heatstroke and should not be exercised in very hot weather. This also makes it near-impossible for this dog to swim, for which reason it should be kept away from deep water. Its exercise needs are moderate, and although it is a game walker, the French Bulldog shouldn't be required to do too much hard running, as one of the few problems it can suffer from is unstable knee joints. This breed is usually easygoing and mellow by nature, and is not normally aggressive either with unknown people or strange dogs—although it can be quite noisy and, for its size, is an effective guard.

EARS Very large and upright "bat" ears, narrowing from a broad base to a rounded tip. Set high on the skull, and turned to the front.

HEAD Square-shaped and big, with a short muzzle and loose skin all over the head, forming wrinkles on the forehead and around the nose.

TAIL Naturally short (not docked) and usually screw in shape (with a slight twist, although not a full curl); there are some dogs that are exceptions to this and which carry their very short tails straight.

EYES Dark and round, set in dark rims and well down the face, below a high forehead. Prominent, but not protruding, and with a calm but alert expression characteristic of the dog's nature.

LEGS Stout and set rather to the sides of the chest, giving the dog a foursquare, stolid appearance.

CHEST A barrel chest— deep, broad, and very well-rounded.

ESSENTIALS EXERCISE 🐾 🐾 GROOMING 🐾 EASY TO TRAIN 🐾 🐾 🐾 EXPENSIVE TO KEEP 🐾 🐾

Standard Poodle

STANDARD POODLE FACTS

SIZE Dog or bitch, height at shoulder, 15½–24 in (40–61 cm).

APPEARANCE The largest of the three varieties of poodle, the Standard is a well-set up, balanced, active dog.

COAT Very thick, dense and curly, in solid shades of black, cream, fawn, apricot, and gray.

BREED HEALTH This breed's popularity has led to some inherited problems, as well as certan non-inherited conditons, including epilepsy, skin allergies, hip dysplasia, and bloat. Standard Poodles should be bought only from a reputable, careful breeder.

AN OWNER NEEDS... The time to meet this lively dog's exercise needs, and the commitment to have it regularly clipped—even those poodles that are clipped to a uniform, short length need professional grooming.

To those who have seen it only in its extreme show clip, it can come as a surprise that the Poodle was, and is, a very capable working dog. First bred as a water retriever, these days it is usually a family pet. A well-bred Standard Poodle is active, curious and outgoing, and good with children and other pets. It needs regular exercise and particularly enjoys swimming and playing in water.

HEAD Long and fine, with an even, tapering muzzle and almond-shaped, dark eyes.

NECK Strong and muscular, supporting the high carriage of the head.

EARS Set at eye level on the head; broad and quite lengthy, and covered with curly hair, with a generous but not over-long fringe.

FEET Oval in shape, small in proportion to the size of the dog, and with compact pads and well-arched toes.

ESSENTIALS **EXERCISE** 🐾🐾🐾🐾 **GROOMING** 🐾🐾🐾 **EASY TO TRAIN** 🐾🐾 **EXPENSIVE TO KEEP** 🐾🐾🐾🐾

Schipperke

The Schipperke was developed in Belgium to guard barges (its name means "skipper" in Flemish), and has been a successful pet as well as a working dog for well over a century. Lively and independent, it can fit in with most lifestyles, but needs plenty of attention and—for its size—a rather surprising amount of exercise. Other than this, it is an easy dog to care for, although the coat moults heavily twice a year, during which times it will need daily grooming.

SCHIPPERKE FACTS

SIZE Dog, height at shoulder, 11–13 in (28–33 cm); bitch, height at shoulder, 10–12 in (25–30 cm).

APPEARANCE An active, little guard dog, with a square outline and a keen, alert expression.

COAT A dense double coat, shorter on the legs and head, with a ruff around the neck extending down the back. Schipperkes are usually solid black, but cream and fawn types exist.

BREED HEALTH Schipperkes are strong and long-lived dogs, but recently the breed has suffered from MPS IIIB, a fatal genetic disorder. Schipperkes should be obtained only from breeders who have screened for this problem in their stock.

AN OWNER NEEDS... To allow the Schipperke to participate in their life 24/7, and to give this endearing little dog plenty of exercise.

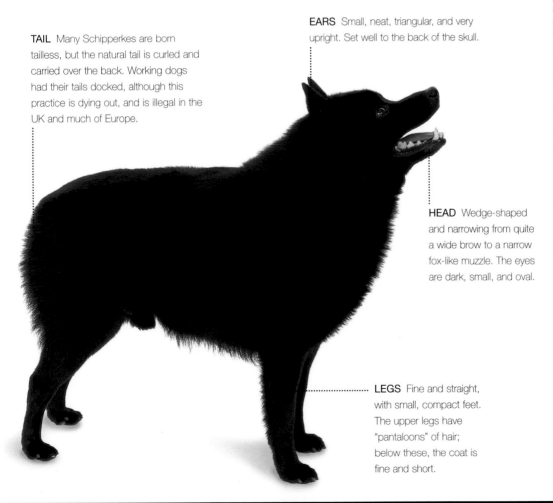

TAIL Many Schipperkes are born tailless, but the natural tail is curled and carried over the back. Working dogs had their tails docked, although this practice is dying out, and is illegal in the UK and much of Europe.

EARS Small, neat, triangular, and very upright. Set well to the back of the skull.

HEAD Wedge-shaped and narrowing from quite a wide brow to a narrow fox-like muzzle. The eyes are dark, small, and oval.

LEGS Fine and straight, with small, compact feet. The upper legs have "pantaloons" of hair; below these, the coat is fine and short.

ESSENTIALS   EXERCISE 🐾🐾🐾   GROOMING 🐾🐾   EASY TO TRAIN 🐾🐾🐾   EXPENSIVE TO KEEP 🐾🐾

Keeshond

KEESHOND FACTS

SIZE Dog, height at shoulder, 17–19 in (43–48 cm); bitch, height at shoulder, 16–18 in (41–46 cm).

APPEARANCE A medium-sized dog of classic spitz appearance, with a solid build and a fox-like face.

COAT A long, straight, somewhat harsh outer coat, standing away from a dense, soft undercoat. The coloring is a mixture of black, gray, and cream over a paler undercoat.

BREED HEALTH Some health concerns, including hip dysplasia, slipping kneecaps, epilepsy, and hypothyroidism. The Keeshond can also suffer from bloat.

AN OWNER NEEDS... To give this dog the personal attention that is very important to it. The Keeshond likes to spend "downtime" with its owners, and isn't good at being left alone.

Originally developed as a guard for barges, the Keeshond is named for Kees de Gyselaer, a Dutch patriot who was on the losing side in an uprising against the royal house in the 1780s. The dog, his mascot, became unpopular as a result, but enjoyed a renaissance in the 19th century, and today is kept both as watchdog (the Keeshond is an enthusiastic barker) and pet. This is a lively, fun-loving breed, but also quite sensitive, so it must be trained gently.

HEAD A moderate wedge shape, narrowing towards the nose, with a darker muzzle and dark "spectacle" lines around the deep-set, slanting eyes.

EARS Of a small, neat, triangular shape, set high on the head and carried very upright.

TAIL Thickly furred and carried in a tight curl over the back, spitz-fashion.

FEET Cat-type feet, small, well-rounded and compact.

ESSENTIALS EXERCISE 🐾🐾🐾 GROOMING 🐾🐾🐾🐾 EASY TO TRAIN 🐾🐾 EXPENSIVE TO KEEP 🐾🐾🐾

Lhasa Apso

Lhasas were first imported to Britain and the United States in the 1930s; before this, it was the tradition for the Dalai Lama to present this little dog (which worked as a guard in Tibetan monasteries) to distinguished visitors as a gift. Lhasas tend to be one-person dogs, and will distinguish "their" person with a show of affection and playfulness. This breed needs careful socializing, and cannot be relied upon to get along easily with other pets or children.

LHASA APSO FACTS

SIZE Dog, height at shoulder, 9–11 in (23–28 cm); bitch, height at shoulder, 8–10 in (20–25 cm).

APPEARANCE A small but stocky guard dog with an alert attitude and an extremely long coat.

COAT A long outer coat of hard, heavy hair, very straight and thick, with a short undercoat, in a wide range of colors, including all shades of blond, grizzle, gray, brown, or white, or any combination of colors.

BREED HEALTH Generally healthy, although Lhasas can be prone to eye problems, including ingrowing eyelashes and inturning eyelids, kidney conditions, and infections of the ear.

AN OWNER NEEDS... The determination to train this determined little dog (Lhasas can be stubborn) and the necessary time to spend on the extensive grooming the Lhasa needs.

HEAD Of medium length, tapering toward a neat but not fine muzzle, and entirely covered with hair, including thick eyebrows, mustache, and beard.

TAIL Heavily feathered, set high, and carried curled over the back.

TOPLINE Straight, and longer than the height of the dog at the shoulder.

GAIT Freemoving, cheerful, and easy, the Lhasa in movement has a jaunty demeanor.

ESSENTIALS EXERCISE 🐾🐾 GROOMING 🐾🐾🐾🐾 EASY TO TRAIN 🐾🐾🐾 EXPENSIVE TO KEEP 🐾🐾

Bichon Frise

BICHON FRISE FACTS

SIZE Dog or bitch, height at shoulder, 9–12 in (23–30 cm).

APPEARANCE A small, sturdy dog with a lavish, fluffy, showy coat.

COAT The truly characteristic feature of the Bichon Frise: a thick, springy double coat, with a soft, fluffy undercoat and a slightly curlier, tougher topcoat, both in pure white, although occasionally with faint cream or apricot markings in young dogs.

BREED HEALTH Generally strong and long-lived, but some health concerns, including skin allergies, cataracts and eye infections, unstable knees, and respiratory problems.

AN OWNER NEEDS... The time to groom their Bichon, or the money to have it professionally groomed, plus plenty of attention to devote to this cheerful breed.

"Bischon" is the French word used to describe a group of small white dogs, of which the Bichon Frise, literally "curly bichon," is the most widespread. Its origins are unclear—bichons have been pets for hundreds of years, and the Bichon Frise probably originated in either France or Belgium. Today, this lively, easy little dog is deservedly popular: playful, loving, and generally friendly towards people and other pets, it can fit in with most lifestyles.

EYES Black or dark brown, slightly rounded in shape, and with a merry, curious expression.

HEAD A slightly rounded skull shape, but concealed by the longer, "powder puff" style of the head hair, a key breed characteristic.

TOPLINE Straight from the base of the neck, then rising in a gentle curve over the hindquarters.

TAIL Set level with the dog's topline, thickly plumed, and carried in a curve over the back.

ESSENTIALS | **EXERCISE** 🐾🐾🐾 | **GROOMING** 🐾🐾🐾🐾🐾 | **EASY TO TRAIN** 🐾🐾 | **EXPENSIVE TO KEEP** 🐾🐾🐾

Finnish Spitz

Although its history is that of a hunting dog, the Finnish Spitz was introduced to the UK and the United States in the 1920s, where it has since been kept as a pet. It is not very widely known, but is regarded as a good family dog; it is particularly fond of children, and will play tirelessly. It is an effective guard, but it needs to be trained to moderate its naturally "barky" tendency.

FINNISH SPITZ FACTS

SIZE Dog, height at shoulder, 17½–20 in (44.5–51 cm); bitch, height at shoulder, 15½–18 in (40–46 cm).

APPEARANCE A well-set-up dog of medium build, athletic, and keen looking and of typical spitz appearance.

COAT A thick double coat, medium-long, with a harsh, straight top layer and a dense, soft underlayer. Colors are solid shades of golden-russet, from pale honey to deep auburn, sometimes with small white marks on the chest and feet.

BREED HEALTH Only rarely has problems, but there are occasional instances of hip and elbow dysplasia, epilepsy, and slipped knee joints.

AN OWNER NEEDS... The energy to train and exercise this athletic and independent-minded dog, and time for daily grooming of its coat.

TAIL Set just below the topline; long, furry, and carried in a tight curl to one side of the body.

HEAD Fox-like, with a narrowing evenly toward the muzzle, with almond-shaped, keen dark eyes and a black nose of medium size.

EARS Typically spitz-type: triangular, high-set, and held upright and mobile.

GAIT Particularly lively, light and graceful, and moving easily into a faster pace. The Finnish Spitz, like most spitz-type hunting dogs, is an endurance runner with an easy, tireless, galloping motion.

ESSENTIALS EXERCISE 🐾🐾🐾🐾 GROOMING 🐾🐾🐾🐾 EASY TO TRAIN 🐾🐾🐾 EXPENSIVE TO KEEP 🐾🐾

Herding Dogs

A straightforward group: as its name implies, all the dogs in this chapter have, at one time or another, been used to herd cattle or sheep. The different methods by which they managed it have led to some very different-looking dogs—low-slung Corgis nipped at the ankles of their charges, while some of the larger breeds served both as guards and herding dogs to their flocks. Most of these breeds need plenty of exercise, and some need plenty of mental stimulation as well.

German Shepherd

GERMAN SHEPHERD FACTS

SIZE Dog, height at shoulder, 24–26 in (61–66 cm); bitch, height at shoulder, 22–24 in (56–61 cm).

APPEARANCE Balanced, well-muscled body, longer than the dog is high. Substantial and deep-chested, with a muscular, well-proportioned neck and a broad, bushy tail carried low with a slight curve.

COAT A thick double coat of medium length. Various colors are allowed in the breed standard, with the darker shades preferred. Pale colors or blue in the coat are considered faults.

BREED HEALTH This breed has a susceptibility to hip dysplasia, eczema, and eye problems. Poorly bred German Shepherds may have problems with aggression.

AN OWNER NEEDS... Confidence and strong leadership to demonstrate to this strong-minded dog that they are worth following: a companion dog without peer, its respect must be earned. Also the German Shepherd needs space, plenty of exercise and mental stimulation.

A well-trained and socialized German Shepherd makes a great pet and a devoted canine friend—smart, tolerant, energetic, and self-confident. However this intelligent dog will run rings around a weak-willed owner, so it is not a great choice for anyone who is inexperienced or inactive. As its name suggests, the German Shepherd was bred to herd sheep, and needs plenty of activity, both mental and physical, to bring out the best in its personality.

This dog is a natural for obedience classes and agility training, and is a companion bar none when you have earned its respect.

Bred during the 19th century from a variety of indigenous German sheepdogs, the German Shepherd had taken on the elegant form we are familiar with today by the early 1900s. Because of its highly trainable nature and its flexibility, it has become popular as a working dog in a wide range of roles, from police dog to guide dog for the blind. Its powerful physique—and its sheer size—make it essential that this dog is thoroughly trained from puppyhood, and good, consistent training will also eliminate any tendency to shyness or timidity. Cheerful confidence is the keynote of a good German Shepherd's character.

This is one breed in which the differences between the dog and the bitch are marked in appearance: dogs look definitely "masculine" and bitches "feminine." The breed standard requires that the German Shepherd's head be "noble," and while the quality may be difficult to define, it's a look that enthusiasts will recognize immediately. It is carried forward on a relatively long neck. The shoulders drop in a slight curve to a strong, straight back, while the power of the dog's outline is carried in the forequarters and chest: side-on, the impression is one of both balance and power.

The German Shepherd needs to be kept busy—long, regular walks are essential, and plenty of time should also be spent on training. It is too large to be confined in small spaces, so a large, secure outdoor space is also desirable. This dog will do best with an equally strong-minded owner who is also active. Properly trained, the German Shepherd makes a good family dog.

EARS Very large, pointed, and mobile. Carried upright, set with the lower corner level with the eyes, and forward facing. Floppy ears are a breed fault.

EYES Medium in size, almond-shaped, dark and expressive, and set at a slight angle in the face.

TAIL Carried in a slight curve, long, broad and tapering only slightly from the base. Bushy, and set quite low.

HEAD Strong, clean-cut, and noble. The muzzle should be strong and long, without any tendency to narrowness. The nose is large and black.

TOPLINE The German Shepherd's line has a characteristic curve, moving down from a strong neck through a straight back to slightly lower muscular hindquarters.

COAT Thick and shiny, with a dense, soft undercoat and a longer, coarser topcoat. The German Shepherd often has "saddle" markings in a darker color over the back.

ESSENTIALS EXERCISE 🐾🐾🐾🐾 GROOMING 🐾🐾🐾 EASY TO TRAIN 🐾🐾🐾 EXPENSIVE TO KEEP 🐾🐾🐾

Border Collie

BORDER COLLIE FACTS

SIZE Dog, height at shoulder, 19–22 in (48–56 cm); bitch, height at shoulder, 18–21 in (46–54 cm).

APPEARANCE A medium-sized herding dog of distinctly athletic appearance, muscular and lean, and with an exceptionally attentive, focused expression.

COAT Two varieties exist, both with double coats, the rough and the smooth. The rough has a longer coat, which may be slightly wavy, but which is thick and weather resistant; the smooth collie, rather the rarer variety, has a shorter coat that may have a slight ruff around the neck. Almost any color or color combination is allowed in the breed standard, although the most commonly seen are black and white, brown and white, and tricolored coats.

BREED HEALTH A strong and healthy working dog, the Border Collie can sometimes suffer from hip dysplasia, and is susceptible to some eye problems and skin allergies.

AN OWNER NEEDS... To understand that this dog needs not just careful training and rigorous exercise, but also a stimulating job to do. Border Collies are only suitable for extremely committed owners.

Born to herd sheep, the Border Collie has been doing its job for generations. The mix of breeds that went in to making this superlative working dog is now unknown, although it is believed that there may be some spaniel in its ancestral mix, as well as other herding breeds. Intelligent, active, and dedicated to its owners, the Border Collie makes a wonderful pet—but only to owners who are prepared to commit a great deal of time and effort to their dog.

The Border Collie has been sent all over the world as a working sheepdog, so great is its skill. It works instinctively—owners of Border puppies will notice them beginning to "herd," crouching and directing anything that moves, from a very early age. The breed took part in the earliest sheepdog trials recorded and today excels not only at herding but at any number of agility and obedience classes as a showdog.

The downside of owning a Border Collie as a pet is that they are very demanding of their owners. Border Collies need plenty of energetic exercise, but they also need mental stimulation, and without a flock of sheep for their dog to herd, owners can be kept busy coming up with things that will keep such an intelligent animal occupied. Many settle the problem by entering their dogs in agility or flyball competitions, or by devising elaborate test and tricks to teach their dogs and to challenge their mental abilities. Bored Border Collies can become neurotic and destructive, so it's kindest to seriously consider if you have the time to dedicate to this dog before you get one.

A happy Border Collie, though, is one of the most rewarding pets one could ask for. Whether the "job" it is engaged in is walking the beam in an agility test or catching a frisbee in the park, its concentration and the enjoyment it takes in its work is a pleasure to watch.

In terms of other care, this breed is not demanding. It needs at least a weekly groom to stop its coat from becoming tangled (and it does shed quite a lot of hair). It can also be slow to mature, having a long adolescence that sometimes lasts to its third birthday. Because of this, it may take time to become reliably trained.

EARS Medium-sized and particularly mobile in this breed: they may be carried upright, folded, or fully drop, and are reliable indicators of the level of alertness.

EYES Oval and set wide apart, ranging in color from dark brown to hazel (as here), or blue. Some Collies have wall eyes—that is, one brown, one blue—which is not considered a fault in the breed standard.

HEAD Well-modelled and narrowing evenly and moderately from the top of the skull. The nose color usually matches the main color of the coat.

LEGS Long and graceful in proportion to the dog, and quite fine in shape, although the hindquarters are broad and muscular.

TAIL Heavily feathered, rather long, with a small crook at the end, and carried low, sometimes rising to horizontal when the dog is animated.

FEET Very deep pads on compact feet, developed for vigorous and prolonged exercise. Toes are well-arched and nails are thick and strong.

● **ESSENTIALS** EXERCISE 🐾🐾🐾🐾🐾 GROOMING 🐾🐾🐾 EASY TO TRAIN 🐾🐾🐾 EXPENSIVE TO KEEP 🐾🐾

Rough Collie

ROUGH COLLIE FACTS

🐾 **SIZE** Dog, height at shoulder, 22–26 in (54–66 cm); bitch, height at shoulder, 20–24 in (51–66 cm).

🐾 **APPEARANCE** An elegant herding dog, with a long face, a flowing coat, and graceful carriage.

🐾 **COAT** A full, flowing coat, short only on the dog's face and legs. The fur forms a thick ruff around the shoulders, and the very dense undercoat causes the straight, harsh topcoat to stand away from the dog's body. There are four color varieties: sable-and-white; white; tricolor; and blue merle (a mix of blue-gray and black fur). A short-coated collie—the Smooth Collie—also exists, identical to the Rough Collie in all but coat, but it is much less popular and widely known.

🐾 **BREED HEALTH** Usually hardy, but this breed can be prone to eye problems, hip dysplasia, and arthritis. The popularity of the Rough Collie makes it particularly important that puppies are obtained only from a reputable breeder.

🐾 **AN OWNER NEEDS...** Enough time to train, groom, and exercise this dog. The Rough Collie is sometimes challenging to train; although intelligent, young Rough Collies sometimes find it hard to concentrate on the job in hand.

Often known simply as the Collie, this lavishly coated breed has a smooth-coated sister type. The two are identical apart from their coats, but for many years the Rough Collie, popularized by the Lassie films, has been by far the better known and more widespread. The word "collie" was originally ascribed to the dog because it was bred to herd the colley (black-faced) sheep of its native Scotland. These days, it is still a very popular pet.

Many of the more functional herding breeds came late to pet-hood, remaining little noticed outside rural farming communities for anything other than the work they did. The Rough Collie is an exception: widely admired for its glamorous looks by the mid-19th century, this breed was a regular subject for artists (especially Victorian artists depicting romanticized versions of the crofting life in Scotland) and Queen Victoria herself raised Rough Collies at Windsor, having encountered and admired them while on holiday at Balmoral.

The original Rough Collies were somewhat shorter and less elegant in line than today's dogs, and at some point in the late 19th century it is believed that Borzoi blood may have been bred in to heighten this dog's good looks. By the 1890s, it was making regular appearances at dog shows in a form very similar to that of the Rough Collies seen in contemporary shows and trials.

The Rough Collie can be slow to train (it has a long adolescence that may last up to the third year in some dogs); with this breed, it is less a case of insufficient intelligence than it is of getting the dog to see the training as relevant to it and its interests. This can usually be resolved by keeping training sessions short and focused, with plenty of treats and positive reinforcement.

The Rough Collie is naturally devoted to its owner and family and prefers to spend its time with them; it is somewhat suspicious toward strangers and for this reason makes an effective home guard dog. It is good with children who respect it, but will not tolerate teasing, having a strong sense of its own dignity.

EARS Small, triangular ears, fully fringed, with the top quarter folded forward into a "V" shape.

EYES Almond-shaped and placed at a slight slant in the face. Brown with dark rims in all colors of collie except for the blue merle, which may sometimes have pale blue eyes or wall eyes (one brown, one blue).

HEAD Tapering to a fine muzzle and relatively slender in comparison to the rest of the dog. The nose of the Rough Collie is always black.

TOPLINE A long back, forming an absolutely straight line from the fall of the ruff around the dog's neck to the base of the tail, which makes a natural continuation of the line.

TAIL Long, with a small crook or swirl at its tip, and heavily feathered. The tail is carried low unless the Rough Collie is excited, when it is held above the topline of the back, but never curled over it.

FEET Small in relation to the size of the dog, with close-set, thick, workmanlike pads capable of going a long way over rough ground.

ESSENTIALS   EXERCISE 🐾🐾🐾🐾   GROOMING 🐾🐾🐾🐾   EASY TO TRAIN 🐾🐾🐾   EXPENSIVE TO KEEP 🐾🐾🐾

Pembroke Welsh Corgi

PEMBROKE WELSH CORGI FACTS

🐾 **SIZE** Dog or bitch, height at shoulder, 10–12 in (25–30 cm).

🐾 **APPEARANCE** Strong and solid, with a long back, large, upright ears, and an active, lively look.

🐾 **COAT** A short, thick undercoat overlaid with a long, hard-textured, water-resistant layer. Colors are fawn, red, sable, or black-and-tan, with or without white markings.

🐾 **BREED HEALTH** The long backs of corgis can lead to back problems. Hip dysplasia and some eye problems are also found in this breed.

🐾 **AN OWNER NEEDS...** A commitment to training this lively dog for good citizenship. This isn't a suitable breed around small children—although corgis generally are particularly fond of them, they nip by instinct and it can be nearly impossible to train them to stop.

One of two very similar breeds of low-slung herding dogs, the Pembroke is marginally the smaller of the Welsh Corgis and is the type that is kept by the Queen. This is a dog with an ancient lineage; there are records of it having existed in Wales since the 11th century. Its propensity for nipping comes from its herding past, in which it rounded up the cattle by biting at their ankles.

HEAD A skull wide and flat between the ears, but tapering evenly down the muzzle, giving the dog a characteristic "foxy" look.

EARS Large, triangular, and carried upright—ears are floppy in puppies and firm up as the dog matures.

TAIL Naturally short and bushy, carried low. Traditionally docked in working dogs, although this practice is now becoming less common.

NECK Substantial, and long enough to balance the long body of the dog and give a symmetrical silhouette.

FEET Paws are slightly oval in shape, and of the hare type. Feet face forward, rather than turning outward.

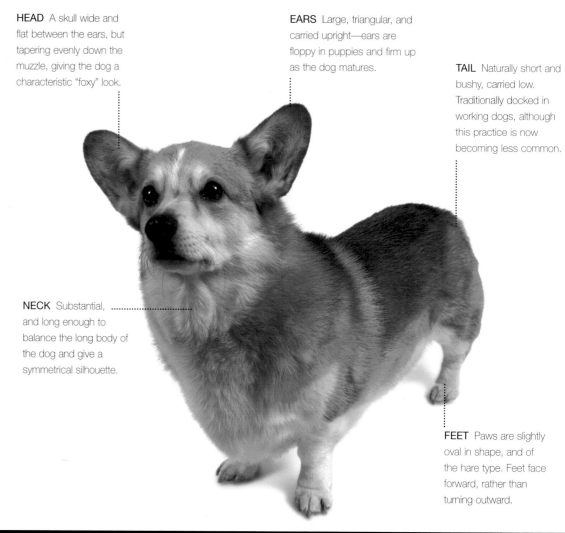

● **ESSENTIALS** EXERCISE 🐾🐾🐾🐾 GROOMING 🐾🐾 EASY TO TRAIN 🐾🐾 EXPENSIVE TO KEEP 🐾🐾

Cardigan Welsh Corgi

Of the two Welsh Corgis, the Cardigan is the less widespread and popular. In looks and character it is similar to its sister type, but is somewhat bigger and with a much longer tail; its personality, too, may be slightly quieter and less cheerfully outgoing than that of the Pembroke. While this dog can be devoted to its owners, it can show some reserve around people it does not know.

CARDIGAN WELSH CORGI FACTS

SIZE Dog or bitch, height at shoulder, 10½–12½ in (26.5–32 cm). .

APPEARANCE Solid and low-slung, with a long body, short legs, a foxy face, and an energetic, enquiring expression.

COAT A straight, harsh outer layer over a soft, dense undercoat, in solid brindle, sable or red, with or wiithout white markings, black-and-tan, and marbled black and gray (blue merle).

BREED HEALTH As with the Pembroke variety, the Cardigan can be prone to back and eye problems and hip dysplasia.

AN OWNER NEEDS... Patience and the time for training. Corgis are intelligent, but need to engage with their owners. They also have a high exercise requirement.

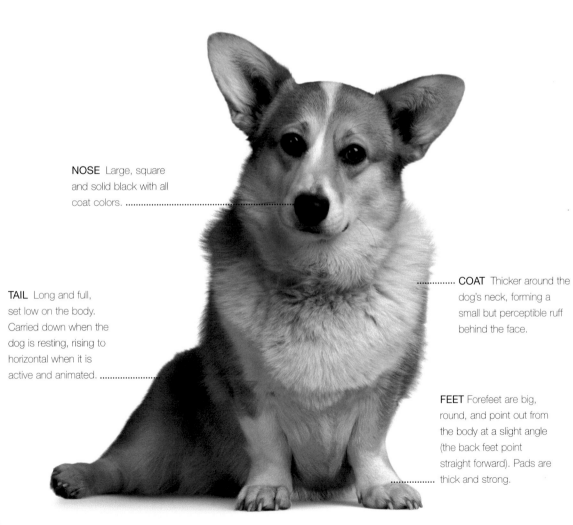

NOSE Large, square and solid black with all coat colors. ....

TAIL Long and full, set low on the body. Carried down when the dog is resting, rising to horizontal when it is active and animated. ....

COAT Thicker around the dog's neck, forming a small but perceptible ruff behind the face.

FEET Forefeet are big, round, and point out from the body at a slight angle (the back feet point straight forward). Pads are thick and strong.

ESSENTIALS EXERCISE 🐾🐾🐾🐾 GROOMING 🐾🐾 EASY TO TRAIN 🐾🐾 EXPENSIVE TO KEEP 🐾🐾

Bearded Collie

BEARDED COLLIE FACTS

SIZE Dog, height at shoulder, 21–22 in (53–56 cm); bitch, height at shoulder, 20–21 in (51–53 cm).

APPEARANCE A long-backed, tough-looking herding dog entirely covered with a hardy, weatherproof coat.

COAT A profuse double coat entirely covering the dog; soft and close underneath, with a long, hard and straight outer layer. Comes in black, fawn, brown or blue-gray, with or without white markings.

BREED HEALTH Beardies are strong dogs, but there is some record in this breed of hip dysplasia, kidney problems, and Addison's disease.

AN OWNER NEEDS... To be energetic and patient enough to exercise, train and groom this exuberant breed.

An old breed that is believed to be descended from crossing the hardy Polish Lowland Sheepdog with the herding dogs of its native Scotland, the Bearded Collie is an energetic working dog that makes an excellent pet provided that its owners have enough time to exercise it properly and to groom its flowing coat. This is a fun-loving but quite high-maintenance dog with a good-natured, lively character. It needs plenty of space, and is not a suitable breed for town life.

HEAD Beneath the coat, the head is broad and square, with a full muzzle and a large, open black nose.

EYES A range of eye colors, from the very dark to the light, usually toning with the color of the coat, and set wide on the face.

EARS Long hanging ears, covered with a dense fringe of hair. They raise perceptibly when the dog is excited.

TOPLINE The back is longer than the dog is tall, and is straight, with no curve up or down toward the tail.

FEET Oval and sturdy, with thick pads, and covered all over with fur, including between the pads and toes.

 ESSENTIALS EXERCISE 🐾🐾🐾🐾 GROOMING 🐾🐾🐾🐾 EASY TO TRAIN 🐾🐾🐾 EXPENSIVE TO KEEP 🐾🐾🐾🐾

Shetland Sheepdog

The Shetland Sheepdog, or Sheltie, bears a strong resemblance to the rough collie, although is a much smaller package. Orginating from the Shetland islands in Scotland, it was bred from working collies, possibly with some Scandinavian Sheepdog blood. Like the Shetland pony, it naturally miniaturized over the years. Although small, this is a tough, sturdy working dog that needs to be kept busy and engaged. Carefully trained, it makes a good pet, and is also often a star performer in agility, flyball, and herding competitions.

SHETLAND SHEEPDOG FACTS

SIZE Dog or bitch, height at shoulder, 13–16 in (33–41 cm).

APPEARANCE Neat and smart collie-type dog with a luxurious coat and a lively, engaged expression.

COAT Double coat, with an outer layer of stiff, straight fur that stands out from the body. Colors can be black, blue merle (a mix of blue-gray and black fur) and tan to deep brown, with or without white markings. Tricolor dogs also exist.

BREED HEALTH Some tendencies to eye diseases, epilepsy, hip dysplasia and skin allergies.

AN OWNER NEEDS... To be prepared to train and extensively socialize this dog while it is still young; Shelties can be shy. They also need plenty of mental and physical stimulation, and exercise.

EARS Triangular and upright, these should show a slight "tip" or fold over at the top when the dog is resting, giving the Sheltie its characteristic slightly enquiring expression.

HEAD A long wedge shape with a gradual taper to the pointed nose.

EYES Large, almond-shaped, and set at a slight angle in the head. Usually dark, although the blue merle coat color may also have blue eyes.

TAIL Long and carried handing down or in a slight curve. The hair on the tail is very dense and long.

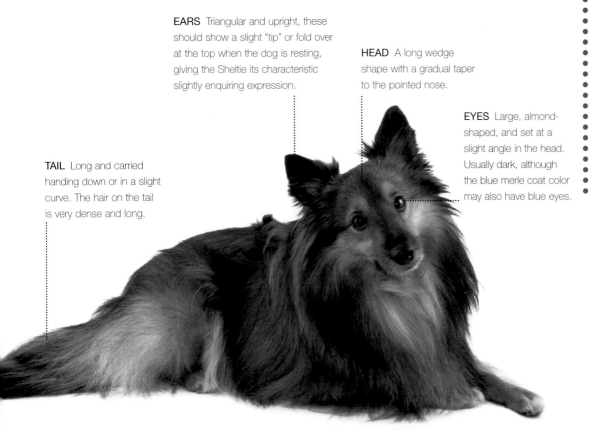

ESSENTIALS   EXERCISE 🐾🐾🐾🐾   GROOMING 🐾🐾🐾🐾   EASY TO TRAIN 🐾🐾🐾🐾   EXPENSIVE TO KEEP 🐾🐾🐾

Australian Cattle Dog

AUSTRALIAN CATTLE DOG FACTS

SIZE Dog, height at shoulder, 18–20 in (46–51 cm); bitch, height at shoulder, 17–19 in (43–48 cm).

APPEARANCE A well-built, sturdy herding dog that is still light enough to be agile in movement, with a very alert, intelligent expression.

COAT A short, dense, weather-resistant double coat, the outer layer lying close to the body and slightly longer around the neck, behind the legs and under the body. The colors are red speckle or blue-gray, which may be solid, mottled, or speckled, sometimes with tan or black markings.

BREED HEALTH Strong and robust, but the Australian Cattle Dog can sometimes suffer from hip dysplasia and eye problems.

AN OWNER NEEDS... The dedication to train and exercise this independent-minded dog and the ingenuity to keep it mentally engaged.

Developed as a tough, hardy herding dog for cattle, the Australian Cattle Dog was not much seen outside its native land before the 1980s, except when imported purely as a working dog. Bred from "heelers," its traditional way of working is to round up the cattle by nipping them. Outstandingly intelligent and very active and lively, it now makes regular appearances in obedience and agility competitions, and is becoming increasingly sought-after as a pet.

Life in the Australian outback called for an extremely tough and tireless dog, and the first herding dogs brought over by settlers were defeated by the harsh climate and the enormous distances they had to cover. To create a dog that could do the job, ranch hands experimented with a number of breeds. The Australian Cattle Dog comes from a very mixed heritage that included the now extinct Smithfield Óeeler, the Bull Terrier, the Kelpie, the Dalmatian, and the native wild Australian dog, the Dingo. This stockpot of breeds resulted in a capable dog that seems to live for work. A breed standard was drawn up as early as 1893 and the dog was officially registered in 1903, but it took another 80 years for it to become known outside Australia.

Enthusiasts for this breed cite its extremely high intelligence and ease of training. The qualities that make it an outstanding working dog, however, make it quite a demanding pet. Like the Border Collie, this cattle dog not only needs plenty of exercise but also an equal amount of mental stimulation to keep it on an even keel: in fact, it really needs to work. What that "work" consists of is up to its owner, who may want to enter their dog in agility or obedience competitions, or simply to teach it a number of complicated and active games. Provided that training is kept equally varied, the Australian Cattle Dog learns easily and with enthusiasm.

Quiet and self-contained, this breed tends to attach itself to one person, although it will be affectionate toward its immediate family. It is reserved toward strangers and needs to be thoroughly socialized from puppyhood to accept new people and to get along with other dogs.

TOPLINE Straight, from the base of the well-developed muscular neck. to a slight downward curve over the hindquarters to the base of the tail.

EARS Medium-sized ears, well-furred both inside and out, triangular and set wide-apart on the head, facing slightly outward.

HEAD Strongly shaped and with some visible muscular modelling around the cheeks. Tapering gently to a powerful jaw and muzzle. The nose is large and black.

EYES Oval and set straight in the head. The eyes of the Australian Cattle Dog are always dark brown and have a watchful expression highly characteristic of the breed.

TAIL Bushy and quite long, set and also carried low, although it may be slightly raised when the dog is animated.

LEGS Both fore- and hindquarters are solidly boned and muscled, but not too bulky or heavy: the impression is one of agility as well as strength.

FEET Round and solid, with short, strong toes and thick, thornproof pads.

ESSENTIALS EXERCISE 🐾 🐾 🐾 🐾 🐾 GROOMING 🐾 🐾 EASY TO TRAIN 🐾 🐾 🐾 EXPENSIVE TO KEEP 🐾 🐾

Briard

BRIARD FACTS

🐾 **SIZE** Dog, height at shoulder, 23–27 in (58–69 cm); bitch, height at shoulder, 22–25½ in (56–65 cm).

🐾 **APPEARANCE** A very large, energetic herding dog, with a powerful, muscular body.

🐾 **COAT** A double coat, the outer layer flat and long, with a slight wave, the undercoat fine and short. Colors are fawn, black, or black with white. The face and ears are often darker in the fawn type.

🐾 **BREED HEALTH** Briards are strong dogs, but have some predisposition to bloat, hip dysplasia, and eye disorders.

🐾 **AN OWNER NEEDS...** To socialize their dog carefully; Briards can be somewhat reserved and should be introduced to a wide range of people and situations while still young. They also need plenty of exercise.

The Briard has been a traditional herding dog in France for centuries, but over the last hundred years has also been widely used in other roles; during the First World War, it was used both as a messenger by the French army and a Red Cross dog. Intelligent, energetic, and not difficult to train, it makes a good family dog and is usually particularly fond of children, but it can be aloof with strangers and needs to be carefully socialized.

HEAD Long, strong, and rectangular in shape. When this puppy is mature, his face will be covered in much longer fur. The nose is substantial and is always black.

EARS Broad and thick, set high on the head and at least half its length. Traditionally cropped to a point, but today more usually shown in their natural form.

TOPLINE The Briard is long-backed, with a slight downward line toward the tail.

FEET Oval, very large, and strong, with thick pads and well-arched toes. The nails are always black.

ESSENTIALS EXERCISE 🐾🐾🐾🐾 GROOMING 🐾🐾🐾 EASY TO TRAIN 🐾🐾🐾 EXPENSIVE TO KEEP 🐾🐾🐾

Belgian Tervuren

The Tervuren is one of four types of Belgian sheepdogs (the other three are the Malinois, the Groenendael and the Laekenois), all of which were originally classified as a single breed. It is similar to a German Shepherd, but in a lighter package. Successful in agility trials, this adaptable breed is an alert watchdog and can be a good pet when obedience-trained and properly exercised.

BELGIAN TERVUREN FACTS

SIZE Dog, height at shoulder, 24–26 in (61–66 cm); bitch, height at shoulder, 22–24 in (56–61 cm).

APPEARANCE Strong and elegant in outline, long-legged and with a handsome, expressive face and an energetic and lively demeanor.

COAT A double coat consisting of a very thick undercoat overlaid with a long, straight top layer. Colors are all shades of fawn, and all shades of tawny and red, overlaid with black, particularly on the face, ears, and chest.

BREED HEALTH Generallly healthy, but Tervurens can have a susceptibility to hip dysplasia, epilepsy, and some eye and skin problems.

AN OWNER NEEDS... The time to spend on training and sufficient exercise. This breed also needs a good deal of regular grooming.

TAIL Thickly furred and carried low with a small hook at the tip. Even when the dog is excited, the tail is not raised above the level of the back.

HEAD Long, with darker coloring than that on the rest of the body. Eyes are dark-brown and almond-shaped, set well to the sides of the muzzle.

NECK The Tervuren has a rather long, well-shaped neck adding to the overall impression of elegance the dog makes.

FEET Tidy, cat-type paws, with close-set toes and pads.

ESSENTIALS   EXERCISE 🐾 🐾 🐾 🐾   GROOMING 🐾 🐾 🐾 🐾   EASY TO TRAIN 🐾 🐾 🐾   EXPENSIVE TO KEEP 🐾 🐾 🐾

Old English Sheepdog

OLD ENGLISH SHEEPDOG FACTS

🐾 **SIZE** Dog, height at shoulder, 22–24 in (56–61 cm); bitch, height at shoulder, 20–23 in (51–58 cm).

🐾 **APPEARANCE** A large, solid herding breed with an extremely heavy and eyecatching coat and a characteristic easy, ambling walk.

🐾 **COAT** A very thick double with an outer layer of shaggy, hard hair that stands out from the body, and a thick, woolly undercoat. Colors can be any shade of gray, blue-gray, or grizzle, usually combined with white, often with a white head, front and paws. The puppies are born darker and the coat lightens as they mature.

🐾 **BREED HEALTH** A strong dog, but it can be subject to a variety of conditions, including hip dysplasia, and cataracts and other eye problems. Some Old English have rather delicate stomachs. This is also a breed that can quickly become overweight if it is overfed, so care should be taken with its diet.

🐾 **AN OWNER NEEDS** Patience to train this sometimes rather slow-maturing breed, and plenty of time to spend with it—this is a very people-oriented and sociable dog that likes to spend a good deal of its day with its owners.

The Old English Sheepdog has been a popular herding breed in Britain since the 18th century; the core stock from which it was originally bred is uncertain, but it is possible that some Hungarian or Russian sheepdog strains were introduced into the native herding dogs of England. Whatever the facts, this solid and utterly reliable dog was recognized as a distinct breed as early as 1888, when the first breed club was established for it.

Also known as the Bobtail, this working dog's tail was invariably docked, although today, many pet dogs keep their long, sweeping tails. This breed worked primarily as a drover's dog, guarding sheep as they were moved from place to place and helping the shepherd to watch over them at night. In this capacity, it had a rather fierce reputation, but today this has long gone, and the Old English is widely regarded as a thoroughly trustworthy and amiable pet.

Large and sometimes clumsy, this breed needs plenty of space, and should also be given regular exercise. The Old English tends to wander and amble, rather than to dash about and use up a lot of energy, so it's a good choice for someone who likes long, leisurely walks

Grooming the coat is demanding, as the double layers can quickly become a mass of tangles without thorough daily brushing. It also sheds heavily and seasonally. If an Old English is a pet rather than a showdog, many owners opt to give it a shorter, utility cut in summer—this not only helps to keep the dog cool, but is also considerably easier and quicker to groom.

In character, the adult Old English is calm, friendly, and very affectionate. It is good with children, and often seems to adopt a guardian-like attitude to "its" family, looking after people in an almost maternal way—this needs to be kept in check if the dog starts to become too serious about it. The breed is usually easy to train, however, and is naturally intelligent. Despite this, it does have a long adolescence; some Old English sheepdogs don't fully mature until they are about three years old, and keep exuberant puppy behaviors for even longer.

HEAD Large in proportion to the dog, with a distinct angle between the upper part of the face and the muzzle, and a strong, square jaw.

TOPLINE Unusually, the Old English Sheepdog has a line that slopes upward slightly toward the rear of the dog.

EARS Set above eye level, of medium size, well coated with fur, and carried flat against the head.

EYES Medium-sized and round, the eyes may be dark brown or clear, light blue, or wall eyes (one eye of each color).

LEGS Very straight and solidly boned, ending in small, neat round feet with compact, heavy pads.

ESSENTIALS EXERCISE 🐾 🐾 🐾 GROOMING 🐾 🐾 🐾 🐾 🐾 EASY TO TRAIN 🐾 🐾 🐾 EXPENSIVE TO KEEP 🐾 🐾 🐾 🐾 🐾

Puli

PULI FACTS

SIZE Dog, height at shoulder, 16–18 in (41–46 cm); bitch, height at shoulder, 15–17 in (38–43 cm).

APPEARANCE A muscular, compact herding dog is disguised by a thick all-over covering of corded hair.

COAT The cords form naturally, and should cover the dog completely; Solid black or brownish-black are the most commonly seen colors, but the Puli also exists in light and dark gray and white.

BREED HEALTH The Puli has few breed health concerns, although there is some incidence of hip dysplasia and cataracts.

AN OWNER NEEDS... Plenty of energy for a large amount of exercise, and the time to socialize this independent-minded working dog.

The Puli hails from Hungary, where it is commonly used to herd sheep, which it controls by running over their backs. Its extraordinary coat is a mass of naturally forming dreadlocks—dense cords of hair that offer protection against cold and damp. Under the fur is an independent-minded and intelligent herding dog that, properly trained and socialized, can make a successful pet.

HEAD Compact and solid, with a strong, deep muzzle and deepset eyes. The nose is always black, whatever the coat color.

BACK Broad, with a straight topline between the base of the neck and the tail.

HINDQUARTERS Very well muscled and solid; the Puli is an accomplished jumper.

TAIL Curled over the body at the back, and with its own dense coat of dreadlocked hair.

ESSENTIALS EXERCISE 🐾🐾🐾🐾 GROOMING 🐾🐾🐾🐾 EASY TO TRAIN 🐾🐾🐾🐾 EXPENSIVE TO KEEP 🐾🐾🐾

Bouvier des Flandres

Originally developed as an all-round working dog, the Bouvier did all kinds of jobs around Belgian farms, not only herding, but also pulling carts, acting as a guard dog, and even following the hunt. It was registered as a breed after the First World War and today is mostly kept as a pet or a showdog. It is intelligent and loyal, but somewhat guarded in unfamiliar situations or with strangers.

TAIL Often naturally short (some Bouviers are born tailless) and generally cropped in working dogs, although the docking of pets' and showdogs' tails is illegal in the UK and some parts of Europe.

EARS Set high on the head, heavily furred, broad but not long. In traditional herding dogs, they were cropped to an upright point.

HEAD Covered all over with thick fur, including a profuse beard and mustache.

FEET Both fore- and hind feet face straight forward and are large and tough with thick pads and well-arched toes.

BOUVIER DES FLANDRES FACTS

SIZE Dog, height at shoulder, 24½–27½ in (62–70 cm); bitch, height at shoulder, 23½–26½ in (60–67 cm).

APPEARANCE A very large and shaggy dog, with a serious look and an imposing presence.

COAT A double coat, the top layer being extremely hard, even harsh to the touch and of an even medium length all over. Colors are solid fawn, gray, brindle, salt-and-pepper, and black.

BREED HEALTH Strong and healthy, but a slght predisposition to cararacts and other eye problems, and hip dysplasia.

AN OWNER NEEDS... The strength of will to tame and train the Bouvier—which can be combative with other dogs—and the energy to give this large breed the equally large amount of exercise it needs.

ESSENTIALS   EXERCISE 🐾🐾🐾🐾   GROOMING 🐾🐾🐾   EASY TO TRAIN 🐾🐾🐾   EXPENSIVE TO KEEP 🐾🐾🐾🐾

New Breeds

Every breed started with a cross between one kind of dog and
another, whether deliberate or accidental. Breeders of long-
established dogs may decry some of these new dogs as "cross-
breeds," but as their popularity increases, the likelihood of some of
them becoming fully accepted, with their own standards and show
classes, also grows, This chapter offers just a·handful of the most
popular of those dogs that are still "in development."

Labradoodle

LABRADOODLE FACTS

SIZE Usually 19–24 in (48–61 cm) at the shoulder, although some cross-breedings with smaller Poodles have resulted in smaller dogs.

APPEARANCE A solid dog with a neat outline, less heavy than that of a full Labrador Retriever and a little less refined than that of a Poodle.

COAT Extremely varied, although usually slightly wavy or curly and with a "woollier" texture than that of a Labrador. Only rarely does the Labradoodle have the fully curly coat characteristic of the Poodle side.

RECENT HISTORY An explosion of popularity has not served this breed well, with some very indifferent dogs being bred for proift without regard to breed faults or qualities. Buyers looking for a Labradoodle should research the dog thoroughly before selecting a breeder.

First bred in the late 1970s, the Labradoodle resulted from a search for a guide dog with a coat that would not irritate allergy sufferers. Crosses between Labradors and Standard Poodles created a dog that was intelligent, easy to train, and with a low-allergy coat. In Australia, an extensive breed program exists, involving other breeds in the quest to create the best Labradoodle.

EARS A medium drop ear, evenly covered with hair and carried close to the side of the head.

COAT A wide range of colors, including blond, liver (as here), cream, silver, and black. Labradoodles usually have solid-colored coats.

EYES Usually dark, although amber is not unknown. This Labradoodle puppy has the rather solemn, soulful gaze that is characteristic of the breed.

CHEST Both the Poodle and the Labrador are deep-chested breeds, and the Labradoodle has the well-developed rib cage typical of both.

ESSENTIALS EXERCISE 🐾🐾🐾 GROOMING 🐾🐾 EASY TO TRAIN 🐾🐾 EXPENSIVE TO KEEP 🐾🐾

Puggle

Enthusiasts for this new breed, which is a cross between the Beagle and the Pug, believe the Puggle holds the best characteristics of both. The longer nose is believed to eliminate the Pug's frequent breathing problems (and loud snoring), while the easy, mellow temperament of the Pug tones down the Beagle's enthusiastic but sometime hyperactive approach to life. Further advantages include the fact that Puggles only occasionally seem to inherit the howling bark so characteristic of Beagles.

PUGGLE FACTS

SIZE Dog and bitch, height at shoulder, usually 12–16 in (30–41 cm), although this may vary considerably.

APPEARANCE A keen, energetic little dog with the solidity of a Pug, but rather finer and lighter lines. The face is an exact mix between the two breeds, with much of the Pug's expressiveness, and its large, round eyes, but a much longer nose, and fewer facial wrinkles.

COAT A short coat that sheds quite heavily. Usually tan with a black "mask" over the face, or pure black.

RECENT HISTORY A very recent breed, which began to be generally known about ten years ago, and thought to have arisen by a happy accident rather than a deliberate experiment. Puggles originated in the United States, and the first to be registered came from a breeder in Wisconsin.

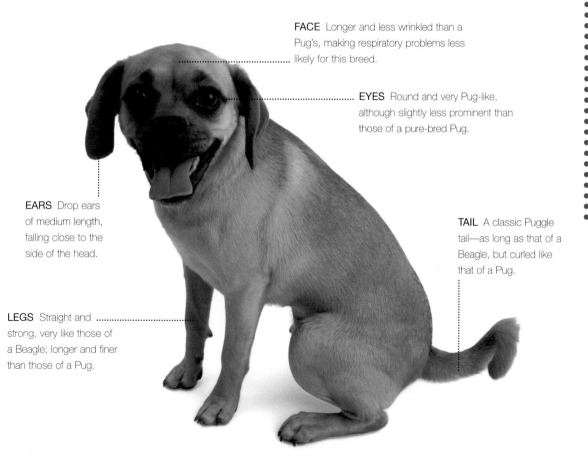

FACE Longer and less wrinkled than a Pug's, making respiratory problems less likely for this breed.

EYES Round and very Pug-like, although slightly less prominent than those of a pure-bred Pug.

EARS Drop ears of medium length, falling close to the side of the head.

TAIL A classic Puggle tail—as long as that of a Beagle, but curled like that of a Pug.

LEGS Straight and strong, very like those of a Beagle; longer and finer than those of a Pug.

ESSENTIALS   EXERCISE 🐾🐾🐾   GROOMING 🐾   EASY TO TRAIN 🐾🐾   EXPENSIVE TO KEEP 🐾🐾

Cockapoo

COCKERPOO FACTS

SIZE Dog or bitch, height at shoulder, 9–18 in (23–46 cm) or more. The extreme variation is because the cross depends on whether the Poodle element in the mix is a Toy, a Miniature, or a Standard.

APPEARANCE This is a solid, squarely built dog with a large, rounded head and an intelligent, lively look. Legs and body are in good proportion to one another, so the Cockapoo appears neither leggy nor hefty, but balanced.

COAT This dog can have one of three different coat types: tight and curly; loosely curly; or flat without curl (the latter may have a slight wave), in almost any color or mixture of colors.

RECENT HISTORY A number of breeders are working hard to get this popular dog accepted as a separate breed. To that end, they have created a "breed standard" for the Cockapoo.

Friendly and amenable to training, the Cockapoo, a cross between the Cocker Spaniel and one of the three sizes of Poodle, has become a popular pet. Size and coat type can vary widely, but this is usually a happy, outgoing dog that is good with children. Easy to keep, the Cockapoo needs moderate exercise and a simple but regular all-over clip for its coat to keep it in good trim.

TOPLINE The line of the back is straight, but with a slight downward slope toward the hindquarters.

EARS Set above eye level, long, and hanging flat and close to the head.

EYES Round and set wide apart; dark brown in dogs with dark noses, a light hazel in dogs with lighter coats and coloring.

TAIL Long and well covered with fur; carried cheerfully up, level with the topline or higher, when the dog is animated.

ESSENTIALS EXERCISE 🐾🐾🐾 GROOMING 🐾🐾🐾 EASY TO TRAIN 🐾🐾 EXPENSIVE TO KEEP 🐾🐾

Schnoodle

A cross between a Miniature Poodle and a Miniature Schnauzer, the Schnoodle is considered a good choice for allergy sufferers. Most of these dogs inherit the low-shedding coat of their poodle side, and provoke fewer reactions than full-shedding breeds. Schnoodles have all the intelligence of poodles, but it is also claimed by enthusiasts that they have the strong companionship qualities, amounting almost to empathy, of the Schnauzer.

HEAD Slightly rectangular in shape, with a shorter, squarer muzzle than that of the Poodle.

TAIL Usually of medium length, slightly tapering, and covered in curly or wavy fur.

EARS A medium ear hanging close to the head, like that of a Poodle. Schnoodles sometimes display the more upright ear characteristic of their Schnauzer side.

COAT Thick, curly, or wavy, with a fluffy, slightly ragged appearance.

SCHNOODLE FACTS

SIZE Dog or bitch, height at shoulder, around 11–15 in (28–38 cm). However, much larger versions, created by crossing Giant Schnauzers with Standard Poodles also exist.

APPEARANCE This is a small dog of square rather than rangy build, with a rough, "deliberately unkempt" appearance.

COAT Can vary a good deal between Schnoodles; usually of medium length and quite rough textured, with a wave or a slight curl. Colors may be black, brown, gray, cream, or apricot. Schoodles generally have coats of a solid, single color.

RECENT HISTORY The Schnoodle's popularity, combined with the fact that, like other new hybrids, it is not yet recognized by any of the major kennel clubs, means that breeding can be indiscriminate. Research carefully before obtaining a Schnoodle.

ESSENTIALS EXERCISE 🐾 🐾   GROOMING 🐾 🐾   EASY TO TRAIN 🐾 🐾   EXPENSIVE TO KEEP 🐾 🐾

Index